US VS. THEM

US VS. THEM

THE FAILURE OF GLOBALISM

IAN BREMMER

PORTFOLIO / PENGUIN

Portfolio/Penguin
An imprint of Penguin Random House LLC
375 Hudson Street
New York, New York 10014

Most Portfolio books are available at a discount when purchased in quantity for sales promotions or corporate use. Special editions, which include personalized covers, excerpts, and corporate imprints, can be created when purchased in large quantities. For more information, please call (212) 572-2232 or e-mail specialmarkets@penguinrandom house.com. Your local bookstore can also assist with discounted bulk purchases using the Penguin Random House corporate Business-to-Business program. For assistance in locating a participating retailer, e-mail B2B@penguinrandomhouse.com.

ISBN 9780525536451 (international edition)
Library of Congress Cataloging-in-Publication Data
Names: Bremmer, Ian, 1969- author.
Title: Us vs. them : the failure of globalism / Ian Bremmer.
Other titles: Us versus them
Description: New York, New York : Portfolio/Penguin, [2018] |
Includes bibliographical references.
Identifiers: LCCN 2018002952| ISBN 9780525533184 (hardback) |
ISBN 9780525533191 (epub)
Subjects: LCSH: Anti-globalization movement. |
BISAC: POLITICAL SCIENCE / International Relations / General. |
POLITICAL SCIENCE / Political Ideologies / Nationalism.
Classification: LCC JZ1318 .B738 2018 | DDC 303.48/2—dc23
LC record available at https://lccn.loc.gov/2018002952

Printed in the United States of America
1   3   5   7   9   10   8   6   4   2

Book design by Kelly Lipovich

For Elisa, who can't read this yet

CONTENTS

CONTENTS

US VS. THEM

INTRODUCTION

W hy do Palestinians throw rocks? To attract attention? To improve their lives? To make progress toward creation of a Palestinian state? They throw rocks because they want others to see that they've had enough, that they can't be ignored, and that they can break things. Voting isn't helping them. Outsiders don't care. Where are the opportunities to bring about change? There is nothing left but to throw rocks.

In that sense, there will soon be Palestinians all over the world. Workers everywhere fear lost jobs and wages as a shifting global economy and technological change leave them behind. Citizens fear surging waves of strangers who alter the face and voice of the country they know. They fear terrorists and criminals who kill for reasons no one can understand. They fear that government cannot or will not protect them. Gripped by anxiety, they get angry. To make themselves seen, heard, and felt, they start to throw rocks.

Then the call for help is answered. Donald Trump tells an excited overflow crowd that he sees them, that he sees their enemies, and that only he can take them (back) to the promised land. Senators Elizabeth Warren and Bernie Sanders tell cheering fans that big corporations and Wall Street banks are robbing them blind. Champions of Brexit tell voters they must reclaim Britain's borders and reject laws and rules imposed by Europeans. European populists tell followers they will lead the charge of patriots against foreigners and globalists.

These leaders aren't arguing that government should be bigger or smaller, that it should tax less or spend more. They're challenging the right of "elites" to make the rules that govern our lives. They tell citizens they've been cheated of their chance to succeed, and that the media is in on it. They promise to comfort the afflicted, afflict the comfortable, and burn down the houses of power.

We can attack these populists, mock them, or dismiss them, but they know something important about the people they're talking to, and they understand that many people believe that "globalism" and "globalization" have failed them. These would-be leaders have a talent for drawing boundaries between people. They offer a compelling vision of division, of "us vs. them," of the worthy citizen fighting for his rights against the entitled or grasping thief. Depending on the country and the moment, "them" may mean rich people or poor people, foreigners or religious, racial, and ethnic minorities. It can mean supporters of a rival political party or people who live in a different part of the country. It can mean politicians, bankers, or reporters. However applied, it's a tried-and-true political tool.

This book is not about the rocks or the damage they do on impact. Rocks are expressions of frustration. They don't solve problems. Instead, we must look more closely at the deeper sources of these frustrations, at how governments around the world are likely to respond to them, and how political leaders, institutions, companies, schools, and citizens can work together to make things better.

There was no wealth where I grew up in Chelsea, Massachusetts, but from my childhood street you could see it in Boston's green and gold skyline. I had no idea what went on inside those towers, but they had my attention. How do you get from here to there, I wondered? When my high school offered a program called "Teach a Kid How America Works," I leaped at the chance to join. We junior achievers put on our coats and ties, headed downtown, up the crowded streets, past the men in suits, through the tall glass doors, up the quiet elevator before gliding to a silent stop, waiting, and stepping into the place where the executives worked. I think it was a bank. It had the deepest carpet I'd ever seen.

Then we were ushered in for an audience with Tim, a man who seemed genuinely glad to meet us. He had a strong handshake, and he looked at me like he was really looking at me. "Would you like to work here?" he asked the group. One of us said yes and the rest nodded in agreement. "Nobody's stopping you, and don't let anyone tell you otherwise. If you want to be successful, you just have to study hard and work hard. It's totally up to you." He believed it, so I did too.

He was right. From the projects, I earned a college scholarship and then a PhD, got an idea, launched a company, made money, got on TV, and wrote books. A kid born on the hard edge of a great American city, the child of a single mother (my dad died when I was four) who, with uncommon singleness of purpose, walked two boys past every trap and pushed us toward success. One small example of the American dream.

As a young adult, the American dream came wrapped in a package of "globalism," a belief in universal interdependence and international exchange that seemed to provide paths to prosperity for both the poor boy I was and the successful man I hoped to become. Globalism seemed a *generous* choice; it's the game everyone can win. Embrace capitalism, lower the walls, hire, build, and expand. People who've made it, or who believe they'll get a fair shot, are drawn to globalism. I devoted my professional life to it. Why not? The system worked for me, and it has lifted hundreds of millions around the world from poverty. Why can't it one day work for everyone?

It didn't, and it hasn't. An early counterexample came with the rioting at the 1999 meeting of the World Trade Organization, where what began as a peaceful, well-organized, pro-labor protest became a magnet for anticorporate, antinuclear, anti-what-else-ya-got anarchist street theater, and then a running battle between kids dodging rubber bullets and cops dodging rocks. Globalists didn't pay much attention. In retrospect, it was a warning sign.

In 2008, years of deregulation, bad bets, and bad faith brought down some of the world's biggest banks, sending shock waves around the world. Next came the Occupy Wall Street movement, leaving bankers worried that the vagrants might get violent. The World Economic Forum at Davos that year was fascinating. No one knew how bad things would get for the global economy or what would happen next. But then came the bailouts for banks, which stabilized the markets. China's leaders injected billions to keep China's economic engine humming, the world's elites went back to business, and Wall Street's occupiers went home.

The Arab world's aborted revolutions got our attention, and the refugee crises it triggered brought them closer to home, but it wasn't until Britain voted to leave the European Union that the indictment of globalism became unavoidably obvious. Then Donald J. Trump was elected president of the United States.

Today, the watchword is inequality. We have always known the world remained an unfair place, but most of the world's elites believed, with plenty of evidence, that globalism was the solution, not the problem. But while the elites convene for debate, more people are getting frustrated.

Back in Chelsea, in my old neighborhood, people are angry. They no longer believe that hard work and education are enough. They don't see a path, and they feel they've been lied to. For decades. My brother voted for Donald Trump, and if my mother were alive, I bet she would have too. She certainly wouldn't have voted for anyone who has spent any time in Washington over the past thirty years. The anger is becoming more obvious—in Appalachia, in Gaza, in Latin America, in North Africa, and in Eastern Europe.

Are the globalists scared? Absolutely not. The United States and global economies surged in 2017 and 2018, and there is no looming global revolution, no World War III that will force change on us all. Public anger is a chronic condition we've learned to live with because the current system works so well for us. What was it Candidate Obama said? In times of trouble, people who have lost their livelihoods "get bitter, they cling to guns or religion or antipathy to people who aren't like them or anti-immigrant sentiment or antitrade sentiment as a way to explain their frustrations." Globalists see enough truth in that statement that there's no need to look more closely at those people's lives. We don't see trade and immigrants as they do, and we don't feel we need to. That's why this problem of broken promises won't soon be solved. It's going to get worse. And not just in the United States.

This book is about the consequences. When human beings feel threatened, we identify the danger and look for allies. We use the enemy, real or imagined, to rally friends to our side. This book is about ongoing political, economic, and technological changes around the world and the widening divisions they will create between the next waves of winners and losers. It's about the ways in which people will define these threats as fights for survival that pit various versions of "us" against various forms of "them." It's about the walls governments will build to protect insiders from outsiders and the state from its people.

And it's about what we can do about it.

CHAPTER 1

WINNERS AND LOSERS

I am the master of my fate,
I am the captain of my soul.

—WILLIAM ERNEST HENLEY

"It's time for a local revolution," the candidate told the roaring crowd. "Countries are no longer nations but markets. Borders are erased. . . . Everyone can come to our country, and this has cut our salaries and our social protections. This dilutes our cultural identity."[1] Marine Le Pen's four sentences capture every important element of the anxiety rising across the Western world. The borders are open, and the foreigners are coming. They will steal your job. They will cost you your pension and your health care by bankrupting your system. They will pollute your culture. Some of them are killers. Le Pen fell short in her bid to become France's president in 2017, but her message remains compelling for the twenty-first-century politics of us vs. them.

But this is not a story about Marine Le Pen or Donald J. Trump or any of the other populist powerhouses who have emerged in Europe and the United States in recent years. Spin the camera toward the furious crowd—there's the real story. It's not the messenger that drives this movement. It's the fears, often, if not always, justified, of ordinary people—fears of lost jobs, surging waves of strangers, vanishing national identities, and the incomprehensible public violence associated with terrorism. It's the growing doubt among citizens that government can protect them, provide them with opportunities for a better life, and help them remain masters of their fate.

As of December 2015, just 6 percent of people in the United States, 4 percent in Germany, 4 percent in Britain, and 3 percent in France believe "the world is getting better."[2] The pessimistic majority suspects that those with power, money, and influence care more about their cosmopolitan world than they do about fellow citizens. Many citizens of these countries now believe that globalization works for the favored few but not for them.

They have a point.

Globalization—the cross-border flow of ideas, information, people, money, goods, and services—has resulted in an interconnected world where national leaders have increasingly limited ability to protect the lives and livelihoods of citizens. In the digital age, borders no longer mean what citizens think they mean. In some ways, they barely exist.

Globalism—the belief that the interdependence that created

globalization is a good thing—is indeed the ideology of the elite. Political leaders of the wealthy West have been globalism's biggest advocates, building a system that has propelled ideas, information, people, money, goods, and services across borders at a speed and on a scale without precedent in human history.

Sure, more than a billion people have risen from poverty in recent decades, and economies and markets have come a long way from the financial crisis. But along with new opportunities come serious vulnerabilities, and the refusal of the global elite to acknowledge the downsides of the new interdependence confirms the suspicions of those losing their sense of security and standard of living that elites in New York and Paris have more in common with elites in Rome and San Francisco than with their discarded countrymen in Tulsa, Turin, Tuscaloosa, and Toulon. "The globalists gutted the American working class and created a middle class in Asia," former White House strategist Steve Bannon told the *Hollywood Reporter* a few days after Donald Trump's 2016 election victory. "The issue now is about Americans looking to not get fucked over."[3]

In the United States, the jobs that once lifted generations of Americans into the middle class—and kept them there for life—are vanishing. Crime and drug addiction are rising. While 87 percent of Chinese and 74 percent of Indians told pollsters in 2017 that they believe their country is moving "in the right direction," just 43 percent of Americans said the same.[4]

In Europe, the European Commission and the unelected bureaucrats who enforce its rules have legislated for its twenty-eight member nations without understanding their varied needs. In recent years, they've failed to halt a debt crisis that forced many Europeans to accept lower wages, higher prices, later retirement, less generous pensions, and an uncertain future, all while telling them they must bail out foreign countries that have spent their way into debt. In the migrant crisis, globalist European leaders insisted that all EU members must accept Muslim refugees in numbers determined in Brussels, and barricades and a spike in nationalism were the result (I define "nationalism" as one form of us vs. them intended to rally members of one nation against those of other nations).

Were the wave of populist nationalism sweeping the United States and Europe the only signs of globalism's failure, it would be bad enough. But there's a larger crisis coming. Many of the storms creating turmoil in the U.S. and Europe—particularly technological change in the workplace and broader awareness of income inequality—are now headed across borders and into the developing world, where governments and institutions aren't ready. Developing countries are especially vulnerable, because the institutions that create stability in developing countries are not as sturdy, and social safety nets aren't nearly as strong as in the United States and European Union. They face an even bigger gap between rich and poor, and the reality that new technologies will kill large numbers of the jobs that lifted expectations for a better life will be much harder to manage. In short, just as the financial crisis had a cascading effect through financial markets and real economies around the world, so the sources of anger convulsing Europe and America will send shock waves through dozens of other countries. Some will absorb these shocks. Some of them won't. As poorer people in developing countries become more aware of what they're missing or losing—quality housing, education, jobs, health care, and protection from crime—many will pick up rocks.

It is not rising China, a new Cold War, the future of Europe, or the risk of a global cyberconflict that will define our societies. It's the efforts of the losers not to get "fucked over," and the efforts of the winners to keep from losing power. Not just in the United States and Europe, but in the developing world too, there will be a confrontation within each society between winners and losers.

And winners and losers there will be. It's too late to assuage the anger of people whose needs have been neglected for years, too late to stop the technological advances that will exacerbate the inequality and nativism stirred up by globalism. What remains to be seen is who will win—and who will be the scapegoat. In some countries, us vs. them will manifest as the citizens versus the government. In other countries, the division will be between the rich and the poor. In some cases, disgruntled citizens will blame immigrants for their problems, punishing "them." And in other cases, an ethnic majority will turn on an internal ethnic minority, blaming them for the problems.

"Us vs. them" is a message that will be adopted by both the left and the right. Antiglobalists on the left use "them" to refer to the governing elite, "big corporations," and bankers who enable financial elites to exploit the individual worker or investor. These are the messages we hear from Senator Bernie Sanders and Greek Prime Minister Alexis Tsipras. Antiglobalists on the right use "them" to describe governments that cheat citizens by offering preferential treatment to minorities, immigrants, or any other group that receives explicit protection under the law.

How will governments choose to react? The weakest will fall away, leaving us with more failed states, like Syria and Somalia. Those still hoping to build open societies will adapt to survive, attempting to rewrite social contracts to create new ways to meet the needs of citizens in a changing world. And many governments that have a stronger grip on power will build walls—both actual and virtual—that separate people from one another and government from citizens.

We can no more avoid these choices than the world can avoid climate change, and the time is now to begin preparing for a world of higher tides. This is the coming crisis. This is the conflict that will unravel many societies from within.

HOW DID WE GET HERE?

In Europe and the United States, the battle of nationalism vs. globalism has deep historical roots, but recent history has given it a new intensity. First, there was the earthquake. The financial crisis of 2008–2009 drove anti-EU fury in response to bailouts and austerity in Europe and resentment of Wall Street and its political enablers in the United States. In the United States, the right dismissed the Occupy Wall Street movement as a vapid left-wing fringe group without significance. The left waved off the Tea Party movement as a motley assortment of angry, aging racists intent on "making America white again" and well-heeled Republican Party activists disguised as grassroots patriots. Other Americans ignored both sides as if nothing important was shifting in American politics. The migrant crisis and a series of terrorist attacks then boosted a more xenophobic set of politicians and political parties in Europe. A number of EU member states established temporary border controls, and some openly defied EU rules. Britons voted to take back control of their laws and borders in 2016, and Trump was elected president as a battering ram against globalist elites and the media in the United States.

Then the anger seemed to abate, and we experienced an illusion of moderation. Barricades in the Balkans and a deal between the EU and Turkey to sharply slow the flow of migrants into Europe eased the refugee crisis and pressure across the continent for another round of border controls.[5] Anti-Muslim firebrand Geert Wilders finished second in Dutch elections in March 2017. Two months later, pro-EU newcomer Emmanuel Macron overcame the challenge from Le Pen to become France's president, though the broader election story was the sound defeat of traditional parties of the center-right and center-left that had dominated French politics for decades in favor of a candidate who, like Trump, had never before run for office.

The center-left showed renewed strength in Britain, though it relied on large numbers of working-class Brexit voters for its revival. Germany's Angela Merkel, defender of European unity, won a fourth term as chancellor. In the United States, the Trump backlash went into high gear. The new president's approval rating settled into a narrow range between the mid-30s and low 40s, and his legislative agenda stalled. Courts blocked some of his plans, and various scandal investigations kept him distracted, though Democrats found no credible message of their own for U.S. voters.

The next chapter is now being written, and it will not be a better one. That's because globalism contains the seeds of its own destruction: Even as it makes the world better, it breeds economic and cultural insecurity, and when people act out of fear, bad things happen.

ECONOMIC INSECURITY

Globalization creates new economic efficiency by moving production and supply chains to parts of the world where resources—raw materials and workers—are cheapest. In the developing world, the influx of capital from wealthier nations has created the first truly global middle class. In the developed world, this process bolsters the purchasing power of everyday consumers by putting affordable products on store shelves, but it also disrupts lives by killing livelihoods as corporations gain access to workers in poorer countries who will work for lower wages.

Trade has not become as toxic a political issue in Europe as in the United States. In part, that's because the European Union includes so many small countries that depend on trade for economic growth, and exports are a crucial growth engine for Germany, the EU's largest economy and de facto political leader. In fact, its current account surplus, a measure of the flow of goods, services, and investment into and out of a country, topped China's to become the world's largest in 2016.[6]

In addition, social safety net protections in many European countries cushion the blow to workers when they're displaced by trade-related change. In exchange for the higher taxes they pay, Europeans enjoy more generous and longer-lasting jobless benefits than Americans, have broader access to health insurance, and pay lower tuition fees for both first-time and older students. Those who champion trade in the U.S. try to make up for these differences with promises that government will provide those who lose when trade moves jobs overseas with so-called trade adjustment assistance—money, retraining, and other forms of support. But these benefits are easier to promise before deals are approved than to deliver after they're signed and politicians no longer need to keep their word.[7]

Beyond trade, globalization boosts technological change by exposing businesses of all kinds to international competition, forcing them to become ever more efficient, which leads to greater investment in game-changing innovations. Advances in automation and artificial intelligence are remaking the workplace for the benefit of efficiency, making the companies that use them more profitable, but workers who lose their jobs and can't be retrained for new ones won't share in the gains. Technological change then disrupts the ways in which globalization creates opportunity and shifts wealth.

As a result, large numbers of U.S. factory jobs have been lost not to Chinese or Mexican factory workers but to robots. A 2015 study conducted by Ball State University found that automation and related factors, not trade, accounted for 88 percent of lost U.S. manufacturing jobs between 2006 and 2013.[8]

Broadening the effect, the introduction into the workplace of artificial intelligence is also reducing the number of—and changing the skill sets needed for—a fast-growing number of service sector jobs. The consulting firm McKinsey & Company has estimated that 73 percent of work in the food service and accommodations industries could be automated in coming years. More than half of jobs in the retail sector could be lost, and two-thirds of jobs in the finance and insurance sectors are likely to disappear once computers can understand speech as well as humans do.[9] What does that mean for the future of work? What does it mean for the middle class? It means that jobs are eliminated, and the middle class continues to shrink. Though technological change may eventually create more jobs than it kills, there's not much reason for confidence that fired workers will get the education and training they need for to-morrow's more technically sophisticated jobs.

In the world's wealthiest countries, particularly the United States, wealth inequality has steadily widened as globalism has advanced. According to a study published by Pew Research in December 2015, "After more than four decades of serving as the nation's economic majority, the American middle class is now matched in number by those in the economic tiers above and below it." In 1970, middle-income households earned 62 percent of aggregate income in the United States. By 2014, their share had fallen to just 43 percent. The median wealth (assets minus debts) of these households fell by 28 percent from 2001 to 2013.[10] Crime and drug addiction have spiked. Nearly 40 percent of U.S. factory jobs have disappeared since 1979.[11] In 2018, U.S. stock markets hit historic highs as U.S. companies drew record profits, but the American middle class is in real trouble.

In an essay for the magazine *Commentary* published in February 2017, Nicholas Eberstadt painted a vivid portrait of the dire state of America's manufacturing class. Between 1948 and 2000, he noted, the U.S. economy grew at about 2.3 percent a year per capita. Since 2000, growth has slowed to less than 1 percent. From 1985 to 2000, the number of hours of paid work in the U.S. rose by 35 percent, but between 2000 and 2015 the increase fell to just 4 percent. Many American workers have fallen out of the labor force completely and have no plans to return. "For every unemployed American man between the ages of 25 and 55," Eberstadt wrote, "there are three who are neither working nor looking for work." Some 57 percent of white men who have left the labor force receive a government disability check. About half of U.S. men who stopped looking for a job take pain medication every day.[12]

President Trump brags that unemployment will hit historic lows in early 2018, but as Trump himself pointed out during his run for president, we must look closely at how the U.S. calculates its jobless rate. According to the U.S. Bureau of Labor Statistics, unemployment fell to 5 percent in September 2015 and has moved steadily lower since, but there's a very good reason why so many Americans are cynical about this number.[13] If you earn less than $10 per hour and work two or three low-wage jobs to pay your bills, you are considered "employed," even if you still can't make your rent. If you're a construction worker who went unpaid last week because bad weather shut down your work site, you are considered fully employed. If you have a temporary job or part-time job, you count as employed during the weeks you work. Even if you have no benefits or a roof over your head, the U.S. Bureau of Labor Statistics' headline unemployment number treats you the same as a person earning $10 million a year. And if you've stopped looking for work after years of failed attempts to get a job, you're not considered "unemployed." You aren't considered at all. No matter your age or how badly you need work, if you're not actively looking for work, you don't exist in this measure of the nation's economic strength.

Globalization's champions continue to sound the trumpets, and many political officials and business leaders still insist that trade creates jobs without admitting that it can kill jobs as well. In his final days as secretary of state in January 2017, John Kerry used a visit to Vietnam to reassure his audience that Americans still believe in cross-border commerce. "Protectionist trade policies won't work," he told the audience in this state-dominated communist country. A few days later and half a world away, Chinese President Xi Jinping pledged his commitment to promoting "global free trade" during a speech at the World Economic Forum in Davos. "Pursuing protectionism," he warned, "is like locking oneself in a dark room. While wind and rain may be kept outside, that dark room will also block light and air."

Yet a new chorus of angry voices in the United States counters that while globalization has been very good to China—and to American corporations and shareholders—it hasn't done much for the American worker. From both left and right, we now hear that trade ships jobs overseas, leaving workers with no future. "Globalization," says Le Pen, is "manufacturing by slaves for selling to the unemployed." U.S. trade policies, warned U.S. presidential candidate Bernie Sanders in 2016, "have enabled large corporations to shut down in this country, throw American workers out on the street, and move to low-wage nations." Yes, a surge of imports brings lower prices for local consumers, but it becomes harder to afford even the cheapest of products when those consumers have lost their jobs.

In the United States, these tensions began building well before the political earthquakes of 2016, during the financial crisis of 2008–2009, when bankers got bailouts and workers got pink slips. Public outrage extended beyond politicians to the media and to failed CEOs who were offered huge piles of cash just to quit. Anger followed everyone who seemed to live above and beyond the damaging effects of these trends. Trade became a contentious issue long before Donald Trump used it to become president, but his ability to speak plainly and forcefully to voters angry about lost jobs helped him capture the 80,000 extra votes he needed to win Pennsylvania, Wisconsin, Michigan—and the U.S. presidential election.[14] Trump also capitalized on growing fear of both Mexican migrants and Muslim militants to argue for a fortress approach to government, to build a border wall, and to try to close the door on as many Muslim refugees as he could. His "America First" rallying cry was crafted to build confidence that he, unlike his opponents, put their interests above the wealthy and well-connected who built fortunes off global trade and investment.

In Europe, the 2010 debt crisis plunged the eurozone into turmoil. Emergency austerity in some countries, economic stagnation in others, and declining demographics throughout have produced pain and frustration. Citizens of some European countries were told their taxes would be used to bail out workers in other European countries that have free-spending governments. Citizens in the countries that received those bailouts were told that their rescue depended on a willingness to work longer for less generous pensions and services.

People who are afraid for their livelihoods lash out as they look for others to blame for their troubles. And economic fears generally breed a second kind of fear.

CULTURAL ANXIETY

The second way in which globalism creates fear centers on identity. Globalization doesn't just move factory-built products. It also moves *people*, feeding public anxiety by shifting the racial, ethnic, linguistic, and religious makeup of communities, sometimes abruptly. Many Americans believe that some illegal immigrants, willing to work for less, take the low-wage jobs that working-class Americans are trained to do while others live off public assistance paid for by U.S. taxpayers. And as political scientist Dani Rodrik points out, immigrants to Europe, whether from inside other EU countries or other parts of the world, add to anxiety among the unemployed that there will be more competition for jobs and fewer social services to go around.[15] This was a particularly controversial issue during the Brexit campaign, as exit advocates like the Conservative Party's Boris Johnson argued that "uncontrolled immigration is politically very damaging, particularly when politicians promise that they can control it," because it creates "huge unfunded pressures" on the National Health Service and other public services.[16] In other words, the foreigners are coming for both your job and your health insurance.

In the United States, as in many European countries, there's an especially strong sense of national identity based on racial, ethnic, and religious affinity. Two June 2017 reports published by the Voter Study Group, a nonprofit research firm, offer interesting conclusions. The first, authored by political scientist John Sides, found that "nearly two-thirds of Trump's primary supporters believe that being Christian is important to being American. This . . . finding implies a continuing divide over whether members of minority religious faiths, and especially Muslims, can be fully American."[17]

Fears of diluted identity mix with economic anxieties. Despite the Republican Party's traditional aversion to entitlement programs, political scientist Lee Drutman has found interesting data on the movement of a surprising number of Barack Obama voters toward Donald Trump. From a survey of 8,000 Americans conducted in December 2016, Drutman identified a group of voters he classified as "populist" because they were "liberal on economic issues [and] conservative on identity issues." About 28 percent of Obama 2012 voters who qualified as "populist" then chose Trump in 2016. Most of these crossover voters agreed with the statement that "people like me are in decline," expressed strong support for protecting safety net programs like Social Security and Medicare, but also held negative views of racial, ethnic, and religious minorities.

According to Drutman, "We can see that Trump's biggest enthusiasts within the party are Republicans who hold the most anti-immigration and anti-Muslim views, demonstrate the most racial resentment, and are most likely to view Social Security and Medicare as important."[18] And while it may seem strange that voters motivated by racial resentment would have voted for Obama, they apparently believed that the first black U.S. president would protect their pensions and health insurance while Mitt Romney, his 2012 Republican opponent, would roll them back. It is this economic insecurity that explains growing opposition to existing free-trade deals like the North American Free Trade Agreement (NAFTA) and proposed plans like the Trans-Pacific Partnership (TPP).

In Europe, this fear of lost identity and economic insecurity come together with the cross-border flow of human beings. First, the free movement of EU citizens across the EU's internal borders, a central principle of the European Union, brings people with foreign names who speak different languages into the labor force in countries across the union.

The percentage of UK residents born outside Britain more

than doubled between 1993 and 2015, from 3.8 million to about 8.7 million of 65 million people in total.[19] That's a direct result of EU rules on free movement of people within the union, particularly from poorer countries of the east to wealthier countries of the west. "What did Brexit play on?" asked the newly elected pro-EU French President Emmanuel Macron in 2017. "On workers from Eastern Europe who came to take British jobs. The defenders of the European Union lost because the British lower middle classes said, 'Stop!'" Macron told a British newspaper.[20]

Add the migrant crisis that brought the largest influx of homeless people since World War II, many of them Muslims fleeing violence and oppression in the Middle East and North Africa, and Europeans begin to feel much less secure about the future of their nations. Recent terrorist attacks, many of them like those in Paris (2015), Brussels (2016), and Manchester (2017) carried out by Muslims born inside Europe, have added accelerant to the political fire. The financial burden of integrating so many migrants will be hotly debated for years, and many estimates of its size are politicized, but a member of the advisory council for Germany's Ministry of Economic Affairs estimated in 2017 that the cost of integration for Germany alone would top €400 billion.[21] The newest arrivals, in particular, will need access to social services that put considerable strain on welfare systems. In addition, a surge in racism is predictable when white Christian men come to see that they don't dominate the United States and Europe as they once did. Western countries are beginning to look more like the rest of the world, and at a time when it's fast becoming harder for a person without a university degree to earn a living, the suddenness of this trend gives it a new intensity.

More than 2.5 million migrants applied for asylum in the European Union in 2015 and 2016.[22] More than 1.1 million arrived in Germany alone.[23] That's one reason why in 2017 Alternative for Germany (AfD) became the first far-right party to win seats in parliament since the end of World War II. The far right has also made big gains in Austria, in part by promising a tougher approach on borders and immigration. The backlash has transformed the political landscape. Though anti-EU, anti-Muslim nationalists like Le Pen and the Netherlands' Geert Wilders have failed so far to win power, every economic slowdown, migrant controversy, and terrorist attack inside European borders will reamplify a political message that is sure to outlast their personal ambitions.

Antiestablishment parties continue to feed popular fury in nearly every EU country. Their leaders insist that unelected Brussels-based Eurocrats strip EU nations of their ability to defend themselves against all sorts of economic and security threats. As in the United States, European nationalists call for border controls, and they vilify journalists, politicians, and business leaders—groups that Italy's comedian-turned-political-arsonist Beppe Grillo calls the "three destroyers."

In Eastern Europe, nationalist anger and a rejection of the democratic values of the European Union have gained a much stronger foothold, particularly among the so-called Visegrád countries: Poland, Hungary, the Czech Republic, and Slovakia. Governments of all four have publicly pledged to ignore an EU quota system for accepting refugees from outside the union. Slovak Prime Minister Robert Fico was the first to close the door, and Hungary followed suit. Poland's President Andrzej Duda has called for a referendum on the refugee question, which he knows will allow Poles to vote to keep them out. Under the EU quota system, the Visegrád Four were expected to accept 11,069 refugees. By June 2017, Slovakia had admitted sixteen, the Czech Republic had taken in twelve, and Poland and Hungary had accepted zero.[24] The European Court of Justice has ruled that all members must comply, and the European Commission has threatened penalties, but the leaders of these countries, confident in the support of enough citizens to win the next elections, have not backed down.

Social values of openness and tolerance for racial, ethnic, and gender diversity *are* still dominant in Western Europe, but these values are increasingly called into question, even in more tolerant European countries and in the United States. During the migrant crisis in 2015, a poll published in the French newspaper *Le Figaro* found that a majority of people in Western Europe favored an end to the Schengen Agreement, which maintains open borders within an area that includes twenty-six European countries. That total included 53 percent in Germany, 56 percent in Italy, and 67 percent in France.[25] Here again we see a poll conducted at the height of an emergency, but it shows the willingness of anxious people to reject the values said to underpin their societies when they feel they're under some form of immediate threat. Some 68 percent of Americans who identify with or lean toward the Republican Party said that millions of illegal immigrants had voted in the 2016 U.S. presidential election, despite no evidence to support the claim, and 73 percent said that voter fraud happens "somewhat" or "very often" in the United States. Do Americans still put democratic principles before party or personalities? A majority of Republican voters also said they would support postponing the 2020 election if Trump and Republican lawmakers suggested it.[26]

Finally, globalism also inspires fear by enabling connectivity. The instantaneous global flow of ideas and information connects more people more quickly than ever before and gives them new opportunities for education, collaboration, and commerce. But it also gives them more to be angry about, new ways to broadcast that anger, and new tools to help them coordinate protest. It shows them terrorist attacks in real time, stoking fears of unfamiliar names and faces.

In addition, the fragmented nature of the Internet has created "filter bubbles," the places we go for reassurance in the form of ideas and information that confirm our biases and connect us with others who share them.[27] Tell me which party you vote for, and I'll tell you which cable TV channels provide your news, which websites you like best, and which newspapers you trust. This creates an environment in which neighbors receive completely different sets of information about the world and the threats it contains. Add the online algorithms that record our searches, interpret our "likes," and keep us in the company of like-minded friends. Social media allows us to follow those we agree with and ignore those we don't, enabling us to deprive ourselves of opportunities to deepen our thinking and change our minds.

HERE TO STAY

Whatever happens to the current wave of political leaders elevated by public fear and frustration in Europe and the United States, the trends that have given them an audience will only gain strength. Whatever the headlines today, this week, or this year, the battle of us vs. them will only become more intense.

First, there is little reason to believe that a decades-long trend toward greater inequality and a greater sense of economic unfairness, particularly in the United States, will be reversed anytime soon. According to a study published in December 2016 by the independent National Bureau of Economic Research, incomes for the bottom half of earners in the United States remained flat between 1980 and 2014, while income for the top 0.001 percent of the richest Americans surged a jaw-dropping 636 percent. The top 1 percent of U.S. adults earned 27 times what the bottom 50 percent earned in 1981. By 2016, it was 81 times higher.[28] Politicians, economists, and ordinary citizens will continue to debate why that is and whether widening inequality is fair. But no matter who is right, the wealthy are unlikely to persuade those struggling to get by that their gains are entirely the result of superior talent and hard work. That's a problem that will plague U.S. politics long after Donald

Trump has left the stage, and Trump's "tax reform" plans appear likely to make matters worse.

Nor should we expect a sudden narrowing of economic strength between the wealthier countries of Northern Europe, where unemployment is relatively low, and the poorer countries of Southern Europe, where unemployment remains stubbornly high. Resentments over bailouts and austerity will create new opportunities for new politicians to exploit in years to come. In addition, the turn toward identity-driven nationalist politics in Eastern Europe will make it difficult for Germany and France to sell the sorts of EU and eurozone reforms that might make European institutions stronger, more resilient, and more accountable.

Widening inequality further, those who do get work will probably see their taxes rise. The wealthiest companies can continue to use their political clout to push for tax rules that allow them to move money across borders to exploit tax advantages. As Rodrik has written, governments will then depend more heavily for revenue on taxing the wages and consumption of individual citizens.[29] That trend will extend the transfer of wealth and widen inequality further.

Nor is there good reason to believe there will be fewer immigrants in the future. In 2016, there were 65.6 million men, women, and children around the world living as refugees, the highest total since World War II, and the inability or unwillingness of political leaders to do much about it says this problem won't soon be solved.[30] President Trump may build a border wall, in one form or another, especially since more than 70 percent of those who voted for him say they want it, but that won't keep out every immigrant who takes to the road in search of a better life. Nor will it end public anger about immigration when a first- or second-generation American commits a heinous crime or an act of terrorism.[31]

The free movement of people remains a crucial element of the European ideal. Citizens of EU countries will continue to cross internal borders for as long as the European Union continues to exist, and opportunistic politicians will blame them when unemployment is high. There isn't going to be a comprehensive Middle East peace plan or a surge in prosperity across North Africa in coming years that would persuade migrants to surrender the dream of life in Europe. The flow may slow, but they will continue to try to reach Europe, by boat or on foot, and many will bring their children.

There is evidence that inequality is a source of violence. A *FiveThirtyEight* analysis of publicly available data from the FBI and the Southern Poverty Law Center found that income inequality "stood out as a predictor of hate crimes and hate incidents." Data from both before and after the 2016 U.S. presidential election showed that "states with more inequality were more likely to have higher rates of hate incidents per capita."[32] Other studies have found that links between inequality and violence exist in both developed and developing countries.[33] No society will ever be perfectly fair. Inequality of outcomes is a fact of life. But it's becoming increasingly difficult for those falling from the middle class to believe that an equal-opportunity country could produce these kinds of results. Even if you think they're wrong, we shouldn't expect politics to remain immune to the political pressures created by inequality on that scale, and there is little good reason to expect a dramatic narrowing of inequality in the United States anytime soon.

Terrorism is unlikely to subside. ISIS, al-Qaeda, and other militant groups around the world will continue to target Europeans and Americans both at home and abroad. These groups may not occupy large expanses of territory, as ISIS once did in Syria and Iraq, but the defeat of ISIS fighters in those places will return a significant number of radicalized, battle-tested recruits to attack the countries they come from. For reasons both geographic and demographic, Europe is at much higher risk than the United States, but neither can ever fully contain the threat posed by those who would use a car, a truck, a gun, a knife, or any other easily available weapon to kill strangers at random. Politicians will continue to make empty promises to do something about it. They will continue to fail. Citizens will hold them accountable.

Cyberspace is another arena in which government will become increasingly less able to provide basic public protection. During the Cold War, the reality of mutually assured nuclear annihilation made it unthinkable for NATO and Warsaw Pact countries to start World War III. Instead, the people of Korea, Vietnam, Angola, Afghanistan, Nicaragua, and other developing countries paid the price as East and West fought proxy battles against enemies, real and imagined. Today, there is no country in the world that can match U.S. military spending. When Donald Trump became president, he asked Congress to increase U.S. defense spending by $54 billion, an incremental increase that tops the entire 2017 Russian defense budget.[34] Over time, a lower oil price will push Russia's military spending still lower. But attacks in cyberspace are much less expensive and not nearly as dangerous as conventional attacks, because it isn't always clear who is responsible. That's why we can expect a lot more of them—and for their sophistication and scale to grow.

In addition, while nuclear weapons are held exclusively by a few governments, cyber weapons are available to anyone with the skill and ingenuity to develop them. At very low cost, individuals and small groups of thieves, activists, and amateur troublemakers can inflict the kind of harm on the world's most powerful governments, companies, institutions, and individuals that would have been unthinkable a decade ago. That's why it will only become more difficult over time for the U.S. and European governments to protect critical infrastructure, citizens, their identities, their data, and their money against attacks from criminals, anarchists, terrorists, or other governments. It will become more difficult to contain the expanding flow of false information that shapes opinions in the twenty-first century and to safeguard the integrity of elections in open societies. That too will feed the public's sense of vulnerability and create political opportunities for those offering simplistic solutions.

Another factor that's likely to exacerbate inequality: next-generation automation. The technological revolution in the workplace has only just begun. A 2017 study published by the Institute for Spatial Economic Analysis found that nearly every major American city will see half of its current jobs replaced by robots by 2035. It's not a surprise that most of the endangered jobs are in the administrative, sales, food preparation, and service sectors. Truck drivers will become a thing of the past as well. But the study also forecasts that advanced technology will replace workers with machines in the offices of doctors, lawyers, schools, and universities.[35]

Even more sobering is the work of MIT's Daron Acemoglu and Boston University's Pascual Restrepo for the National Bureau of Economic Research. In a study published in 2016, Acemoglu and Restrepo predicted that the net effect of automation and other technological changes in the workplace would ultimately prove positive as they created new kinds of jobs that paid higher wages to replace existing lower-wage work. But in 2017, they revised their views based on more detailed research. They found that industrial robots were responsible for as many as 670,000 lost manufacturing jobs between 1990 and 2007, that this number was likely to rise as the number of robots quadruple in coming years, and that other sectors weren't creating enough jobs to offset the losses in manufacturing.[36] "The conclusion is that even if overall employment and wages recover, there will be losers in the process, and it's going to take a very long time for these communities to recover," according to Acemoglu.[37]

This isn't simply a story about robots sending workers home. As in the past, new technologies will create new jobs—and new kinds of jobs. But the increasing automation of the workplace, advances in machine learning, and the broad introduction into the economy of new forms of artificial intelligence will ensure that jobs of the future will require ever higher levels of education and training. As anyone now paying tuition—for themselves or someone else—knows all too well, the price of higher education in the United States is rising faster than for almost any other service. College tuition has risen by about 6 percent per year, according to Vanguard, a money management fund. If the increase continues at that rate over the next generation, a four-year college degree for an American born in 2017 would reach $215,000 at a public school and $500,000 at a private one,[38] further compounding an already growing student debt crisis in the United States.[39] Those who can pay will get the education, and those with the knowledge and skill set will have opportunities for good-paying jobs that those without them won't have. "If you've worked in Detroit for ten years, you don't have the skills to go into health care. The market economy is not going to create the jobs by itself for these workers who are bearing the brunt of the change," Acemoglu warned.[40]

Human beings want security, opportunity, and prosperity, and governments want to claim credit for providing these things. Both the government and the governed want to believe they have the means to retake control of their circumstances when they believe these things are threatened. This is the battle line between us and them. Nationalism grows from a need to reassert control by declaring shared solidarity. It promises to confront the forces that are believed to breed disorder and that compromise both personal and national sovereignty. It pledges to build strong walls to keep "them" at bay.

Despite much-improved economic performance in the United States and around the world in 2017 and 2018, the battle between us and them continues in every country where fear of change is on the rise. As we'll see in the next chapter, this is not simply a story of Europe and America. This struggle is set to go global.

CHAPTER 2

WARNING SIGNS

It is impossible to predict the time and
progress of revolution. It is governed by its own
more or less mysterious laws.

—VLADIMIR LENIN

For seven years, Mohammed Bouazizi supported a family of eight with cash earned from an unlicensed vegetable cart in Sidi Bouzid, a town 190 miles south of Tunisia's capital. On December 17, 2010, a police officer confiscated his produce and told him he could no longer sell. Desperate, Bouazizi went to the town hall for help. No one would see him. He then drenched himself in gasoline and lit a match. In the eighteen days it took him to die, Al-Jazeera broadcast his story across the Arab world. Public anger grew, and protests swelled. Bouazizi died on January 4. Ten days later, the twenty-three-year dictatorship of President Zine el-Abidine Ben Ali was brought to its knees. In Tunisia, change came gradually and then suddenly.[1]

Across the border in Egypt, hundreds of thousands of angry, inspired people demanded that their government deliver change or stand down. On February 11, President Hosni Mubarak was ousted after three decades in power.[2] Across North Africa and the Middle East, new crowds gathered, and strongmen shuddered. In October, Libya's Muammar Qaddafi was hounded from power, found hiding in a drainage pipe, and bayonetted in the street.[3] Over the next several years, civil war in Syria killed or displaced half the country's population.[4]

In none of these countries did most citizens, particularly young people, believe that government would help them build a secure and prosperous life. Satellite television and the introduction of social media showed them they were not alone and that they didn't have to accept that nothing ever changes. These were not people who shared in the rising living standards elsewhere in the developing world, and they knew it. Just as in Europe and the United States, many of these people came to believe that their countries were governed by elites for the benefit of elites, whether in government, business, or the military, and that no one in power cared about them or their families. They believed that nothing would ever change unless they changed it.

This story reminds us just how quickly public anger can change history, but it is not simply the poor and excluded that governments have to worry about. In many developing countries, governments are becoming victims of their own success.

Those who have joined the new middle class don't just *want* better government; they *expect* it. They demand it. This is the natural result of a larger international success story that is now visible even to those who haven't fully shared in it.

And thanks to globalism's coming tech innovations, the problem will be far, far worse in developing countries than in the wealthy West.

VICTIMS OF SUCCESS

At first glance, the numbers seem to say that globalism has been all good news for the developing world. World Bank statistics show that the percentage of the world's people who live in "extreme poverty" fell from 64 percent in 1960 to less than 10 percent in 2015. In 1960, 58 percent of people around the world were illiterate. In 2014, that number was just 15 percent.[5] Access to education and health care has climbed alongside life expectancy, and the biggest developing countries have benefited most. In India, there were 338 million people living on less than one dollar per day in 1990. By 2013, that number had fallen to 218 million. In Brazil, the number fell from 31 million to 10 million, and in Indonesia from 104 million to 25 million. In Russia, the drop was from 3 million to about 40,000 people. In China, the number plummeted from 756 million to just 25 million, a fall of more than 95 percent.[6] That's a true story, and one that globalization's champions love to tell.

But there's more to the story.

During the first decade of the twenty-first century, a surge in credit markets turbocharged economic growth and created an unprecedented period of abundance in many developing countries. China's rapid rise lifted emerging-market boats as its demand for commodities poured cash into countries on every continent. For oil producers, crude prices well above $100 per barrel brought in tidal waves of cash, allowing state officials to continue to siphon money into corrupt, cash-eating state-owned companies. Boom times secured the power of ruling parties and leaders, but also allowed them to dodge some tough questions. When should we ask a lot more people to pay taxes? When should we cut subsidies on things like food and fuel in a country that still has large numbers of people living hand to mouth? Why shut down unproductive factories and put workers on the streets when we can wait until next year? In short, why mess with success?

Then came the global financial crisis. By exposing the short-comings of underregulated markets and the threats they posed to the economic and political stability of much of the world in 2009 and 2010, market turmoil appeared to discredit American-style private-sector-driven capitalism in favor of a seemingly more stable state-dominated model with Chinese characteristics. Another source of trouble for the governments of many developing countries: The giant was no longer quite so hungry. China's economy has slowed in recent years, an expected by-product of reforms that acknowledge that no country, not even intelligently governed China, can keep a double-digit annual economic pace forever. This slowdown—and China's shift from heavy government spending on resource-devouring infrastructure construction to a growth model driven more by middle-class consumption—means lower Chinese demand for oil, gas, metals, and minerals from other emerging countries. Lower commodity prices, particularly for crude oil, undermine growth in resource-rich developing countries like Saudi Arabia, Russia, Brazil, South Africa, Venezuela, Nigeria, and others.

Around the world, tougher economic times make governments less popular. In response, political leaders then spend too much money, including on subsidies. They pressure central banks to print more money to stimulate an economy in the short term, stoking inflation and raising public anxiety as cash buys less than it did the week before. They block foreign investment to protect local interests, workers, and sectors, exacerbating long-term problems by making their economies less competitive.

Even without the coming tech change, frustrations are high in many developing countries. Globalization created rapid industrialization, and the resulting filthy air and water can drive protest as well. In December 2016, residents of the smog-blanketed southwestern Chinese city of Chengdu began placing pollution masks on statues in the city center. Police in riot gear responded to a gathering in the city's Tianfu Square with a crackdown that lasted several days. Protesters then took to social media with photographs of themselves holding signs that read "Let me breathe."[7] For years, the Chinese leadership has searched for solutions to the problems of toxic air and water, but plans to shutter economically wasteful and polluting industries push miners and steelworkers out of their jobs, sending new groups of disgruntled citizens into the streets. Every road leads to potential trouble.

The Chinese government, which has managed the political risk that flows from public protests as efficiently as any authoritarian government in the world since the Tiananmen Square crackdown in June 1989, once published a statistic on the number of the country's "mass incidents," or protests that involve at least a few dozen people. (The minimum threshold has varied over time from about fifty to one hundred people.) A few have involved thousands. According to official Chinese figures, the number of these protests grew from about 8,700 in 1993 to more than 127,000 in 2010.[8] The state no longer publishes this number, but there's no reason to believe there aren't still large numbers of public protests each year, particularly because these stats are politically ultra sensitive. The sources of public anger include local corruption, environmental worries, ethnic tensions, lost jobs, product safety problems, and even spontaneous explosions of rage that can arise from a simple traffic accident. As in Russia, protests in China pose virtually no near-term threat to the Communist Party's monopoly hold on political power. China's leaders remain firmly in charge, but they know there will be plenty of complicated and dangerous challenges ahead.

In another example of pollution fears launching a near revolution, take Turkey. On May 27, 2013, a group of environmental activists gathered in Istanbul's Gezi Park to protest government plans to uproot a grove of trees in the city's central district to clear space for a shopping mall. Their aim was to occupy the park to block the work. The next day, police moved in with tear gas and pepper spray to break up their camp. Coverage on social media included violent images from the confrontation, and the numbers of both protesters and police began to grow. As anger intensified, protesters spilled into the streets of Izmir, Ankara, and other Turkish cities. Thousands were injured and hundreds arrested across dozens of Turkish provinces. Some were charged with crimes for writing posts about the protests on Twitter.[9] On June 4, a protester was killed.[10]

On June 13, then Prime Minister Recep Tayyip Erdogan issued a final warning for protesters to leave the park.[11] The violence escalated, and more protesters died. Turkey's Interior Ministry reported on June 23 that about 2.5 million people had taken part in demonstrations in seventy-nine of the country's eighty-one provinces.[12] The fury continued for weeks. By the time the storm had subsided, eight people were dead and about eight thousand were injured.[13] What had begun as an environmental protest became a stand against police brutality fueled by frustration with an increasingly authoritarian government. In 2016, a failed coup attempt against now President Erdogan further polarized this already divided country, and Erdogan's bid to grant himself ever expanding Vladimir Putin–scale powers has deepened the public indignation that a big segment of Turkey's people now feel toward their government.

In other countries, frustration boils over as the contracting economy forces the government to provide less for their now expectant people. At almost exactly the same time as Turkey's protests began in June 2013, the city government in Sao Paulo,

Brazil, announced a nine-cent hike in bus fares. The public response was instantaneous. In a country where minimum-wage workers spend a quarter of their income on public transport, protesters took to the streets. As in Turkey, a brutal police response turned a local protest national—and the press coverage went global. Hundreds of thousands of angry people in cities across the country began to protest corruption, lousy public services, and police violence. A sharp economic slowdown and the Lava Jato corruption scandal—the largest in Brazil's history—have made street protest a much more common event in a country mired in a long and deep economic recession. In March 2015, another round of demonstrations brought an estimated 2.4 million people into the streets of Brazil's biggest cities. In January 2016, protests erupted anew when Sao Paulo officials tried again to raise bus fares. In March 2016, some 3.6 million joined new street protests. The demonstrations have continued, and some have turned violent.[14] This is a new development in a country where, until five years ago, street demonstrations were limited mainly to periodic strikes organized by trade unions.

In other regions and in countries with different systems, new protests have emerged in response to various forms of bitter frustration with government. In 2014, in the Ethiopian city of Ambo, university students began demonstrations against a plan to expand Addis Ababa, the country's capital, into the surrounding countryside, forcing farmers off their land. In the confrontation with police that followed, seventeen were killed, and protests spread across the country.[15] Though the city expansion plans were scrapped, hundreds have since been killed and thousands arrested.[16] More of the world became aware of Ethiopia's unrest when, during the 2016 Rio Olympic Games, marathon silver medalist Feyisa Lilesa crossed his arms above his head as he crossed the finish line in a gesture of solidarity with protesters. Three weeks later, fear that dissent would grow out of control led the ruling Ethiopian People's Revolutionary Democratic Front to declare a state of emergency, which remained in place until August 2017.

Much of the hostility in Ethiopia is related to ethnically based political grievances. Members of the Oromo and Amhara communities, which together make up more than 60 percent of the population, have set aside differences during the protests to focus anger at a government that both feel is dominated by minority Tigrayans. But as in Turkey and Brazil, these protests are not the sign of hopelessness we saw in Tunisia and Egypt at the dawn of the Arab Spring. In the decade before 2016, Ethiopia's economy grew at a red-hot 8 percent to 11 percent per year.[17] The country's infrastructure—roads, bridges, electricity, etc.—is strong by Africa's standards. But as in the United States and Europe, globalization has produced losers as well as winners. Youth unemployment in Ethiopia's cities remains just under 30 percent, and many new jobs consist of manual labor that can't satisfy the ambitions of university graduates for a better life.[18] As in Brazil and Turkey, expectations have been raised that citizens can ask more from government. And as in Brazil and Turkey, government isn't keeping up.

In developing democracies and authoritarian states alike, corruption is a familiar complaint, whether at the petty local-shakedown level or at the highest reaches of government. In 2017, demonstrations against state corruption organized by opposition activist Alexei Navalny reportedly included 60,000 people in eighty-two Russian cities and towns from the Baltic Sea to the Pacific Ocean. Protesters carried yellow rubber ducks to mock Prime Minister Dmitry Medvedev's extravagant lifestyle, symbolized by a house built as a waterfowl sanctuary on one of several lavish properties he regularly used. Hundreds were arrested in Moscow alone.[19]

A poll conducted not long after by Moscow's Levada Center found that though 72 percent of people said they trusted Vladimir Putin, 67 percent said he was "fully" or "in large part" responsible "for the scale of high-level government corruption and financial abuse that are frequently cited by his opponents." More than half (51 percent) said they were tired of waiting for him to improve their lives. Just 32 percent said Putin had improved their living standards. That same percentage said their president had successfully fought corruption.[20] As he stands for reelection in 2018, Putin remains popular, and protests will not weaken his grip on power, but even this deeply entrenched and genuinely popular leader must worry about the future.

Pollution, corruption, economic problems—there would be enough reason to fear for developing countries even if the coming tech disruption weren't expected. As it is, many fragile countries are headed for serious trouble.

CUE THE ROBOTS

All these challenges are important for developing countries, but it's the tech revolution that will create unprecedented pressure on emerging states and their more fragile institutions. In November 2016, the United Nations warned that two-thirds of all jobs in the developing world were at risk.[21] While automation and innovations in machine learning threaten 47 percent of all jobs in the United States, the number is 65 percent in Nigeria, with a population of 140 million people, 69 percent in India, home to more than 1.3 billion, and 77 percent in China, a country of 1.4 billion.[22] That's a lot of personal upheaval involving very large numbers of people. Again, the point is not that all those jobs will disappear. It's that, even if one type of job is simply replaced with a newer type that complements the work of machines, the transition will be brutally difficult on a historically unprecedented scale.

To begin to understand the scale of change that robotics and artificial intelligence, in particular, will bring to the political lives of developing countries, look back at their past successes.

Successful emerging-market countries tend to follow a similar pattern of development. They begin as poor countries with large numbers of people living in the countryside. The young begin moving toward cities, where they hope to earn higher wages for themselves and their families. They arrive ready to work, but are in no position to command high wages. This sudden surge of inexpensive labor attracts the attention of manufacturers who own factories in countries where workers are much more highly paid. New factories appear, and word of new jobs makes its way to rural areas, generating an even bigger wave of poor young people headed for the big city. This is now an old and familiar story, one that has played out hundreds of millions of times in China, India, and across Southeast Asia, Latin America, and sub-Saharan Africa.

Problems begin to develop as cities sag under the weight of all these new people. Governments that don't have much money can't afford to build the new roads, bridges, public transport, public schools, and public hospitals needed to accommodate all these new people. Those that can pay the bill discover that investment in better infrastructure attracts even more new people into the cities, demanding still more infrastructure. Those that are well governed can flourish. Those that are poorly governed become incubators of crime, corruption, anger, and protest.

The next stage of development begins as these once poor workers begin to demand higher wages and better working and living conditions. Consumer classes appear in countries that have never had them. Higher pay for these workers means the country is no longer as attractive for foreign companies, but some countries—those with capable, reform-minded governments—can adapt. New technologies—purchased, invented, or stolen—allow them to get more productivity from each worker, who then produces more sophisticated, higher-value-added goods and services that continue to push wages higher. A sea change that began with low-cost manufacturing ends with the birth of a true middle class.

But the virtuous circle that depends on good demographics, labor mobility, economic growth, and political reform is beginning to break down. The global introduction of robotics and AI, even on a limited scale, will sharply reduce the low-wage advantage that helps poor countries and poor people become middle-income countries and middle-class consumers. A shoe manufacturer in Kentucky is better off replacing a middle-wage worker with a no-wage robot than with a low-wage worker in Mexico, China, or Cambodia. And with the advent of 3-D printing, companies can keep manufacturing much closer to the customers who will buy their products. No need to move factories to distant shores.

Where do all those energetic, ambitious young people go? The youth bulge we see in many developing countries can move from economic advantage to political threat as their path out of poverty is blocked. If they never join the active workforce, they will never have access to the education and training needed to earn twenty-first-century jobs, and they know their children will fare no better. Those able to keep their jobs may discover they must work for less pay and fewer (if any) benefits. If automation reduces wages in developing countries, it may become impossible for workers to gain the education needed to succeed in a world where advanced AI generates a much bigger share of the economic growth. Lower growth means less government revenue—and, therefore, less money to spend for education and services, for infrastructure, and for all the other things that middle classes expect from government. The virtuous circle becomes a vicious circle.

In 2018, it's still too soon to know whether the tech revolution will kill more jobs than it creates. But as in the rich countries, we can be very sure that the new jobs will be very different from the old ones, that education and training for these new forms of work will be fundamentally different, and that large numbers of workers won't make the leap from the old world to the new. It's an open question where those who lose from this next wave of change will declare their political allegiance—or whether they will declare war on the entire system. The growing violence we've seen in Venezuela in recent years provides a vivid reminder of what happens when frustrated people have no nonviolent outlet to demand change.

There are many reasons why the tech revolution will hit the emerging world much harder than it will hit Europe and the United States. In developed countries, children are more likely to grow up with digital technologies as toys and then to encounter them in school. Governments in these countries have money to invest in educational systems that prepare workers, both blue and white collar, for change. Their universities have much greater access to state-of-the-art technologies. Their companies produce the innovations that drive tech change in the first place. This creates a dynamic in which high-wage countries are more likely than low-wage ones to dominate the skill-intensive industries that will generate twenty-first-century growth, leaving behind large numbers of those billion-plus people who only recently emerged from age-old deprivation. The wealth in developed countries helps them maintain much stronger social safety nets than in poorer countries to help citizens who lose their jobs, fall ill, or need to care for sick children or aging parents. In short, wealthier countries are both more adaptable and more resilient than developing ones.

There's also an important political difference. Developing countries are politically much more brittle than in Europe or the United States. Governments are more likely to carry less popular legitimacy, particularly if they are unelected. The institutions of government—parliaments, courts, and state ministries—are less well established, potentially more fragile, and less likely to impose useful checks on power. The embattled governments of developing countries are also more likely than those in the rich world to find their backs to the wall, to turn to repression to remain in power and out of jail, to enact policies that generate crises, trouble from which they are less likely to recover, and to concentrate power in ways that make economies more rigid.

It's a reminder that developing countries have a history of populist repression that might be repeated. We don't need to remember China's Mao, Egypt's Nasser, Argentina's Perón, Indonesia's Sukarno, Peru's Alvarado, Pakistan's Zulfikar Ali Bhutto, or Libya's Qaddafi to know that economic insecurity in developing countries creates opportunities for charismatic populists to win votes from "us" by demonizing "them." Think of Turkey's Erdogan, Venezuela's Chávez, or Russia's Putin—a man able to consolidate enormous power by restoring order (with the help of historically high oil prices) after nearly a decade of post-Soviet economic crisis. As we saw in the last chapter, American and European politicians do this too, but the checks and balances of their political systems limit their ability to dominate their countries.

There is another important difference between developed and developing states. In American and European politics, "them" is often an immigrant hoping to come inside—the Mexican or Central American migrant hoping to enter the United States or the Middle Eastern/North African Muslim refugee hoping to live in Germany, France, Britain, or Sweden. In poorer countries, especially those with borders drawn by colonizers, "them" is often the ethnic, religious, or sectarian minorities with roots that are older than the borders themselves. Think of Muslims in India, in western China, or in the Caucasus region of Russia. Sunni Muslims in Iraq or Shia Muslims in Saudi Arabia. Think of Christians in Egypt or Kurds in Turkey. Think of Chinese and other ethnic minorities in Indonesia and Malaysia. There are many more examples. These groups become easy targets when times are hard and a politician looks to make a name for himself at their expense. Rwanda and the former Yugoslavia offer the most important recent cautionary tales of how developing countries with weak institutions can repeat the atrocities committed in earlier eras.

RESILIENCE

What are the factors that will determine how emerging countries and their citizens weather these building storms? First, survival depends on adaptation to change, and governments must have the means to adapt. Those that can't afford to invest in the development of new technologies will see their economies lose their competitive edge. They won't produce growth and jobs, leaving government without the revenue it needs to invest in the future. In particular, some governments that have traditionally pulled wealth out of the ground in the form of oil, gas, metals, and minerals are already discovering that this model won't sustain them indefinitely.

But it's not enough for governments to invest in new technologies. They must also invest in the process of training citizens to use them. If they don't already have strong education systems, from early childhood through higher education, they will have to develop them. Some developing countries will make this leap, and some won't. They must also work with industry to help retrain workers to minimize the number of those who can't keep pace with evolving demand for new skills. They must invest in roads, bridges, ports, airports, schools and hospitals, and the digital-age infrastructure needed to ensure that energy and information flow efficiently.

In addition, governments must minimize inequality. This is especially important in a world where it has never been easier to find out how foreigners live. The point is not to prevent wealth creation or to reward people who have done nothing to deserve help and will probably squander it. It's not a question of equality of outcome but of opportunity, a viable path toward a better life. The larger the percentage of people with good reason to believe that the system will prevent them from bettering themselves, the greater the risk of conflict for which everyone pays a price. As part of this battle, fighting corruption is crucial. If the less powerful have no means to protect themselves when the more powerful strip them of what they have, they will rebel. If ordinary citizens believe the political and economic system exists only to maintain the divide between privilege and poverty, they will find ways to fight back. A basic level of trust in government and its institutions is critical.

Given the changes that automation and artificial intelligence will bring to the workplace, there will be an important change in the relationship between demographics and political stability. As globalization created new opportunities for poor countries with low-wage workers to export products to wealthier countries, surging populations of young people offered an advantage for countries like India and appeared to put fast-aging China in long-term danger. But in a world where new technologies ensure that fewer jobs are created for each new unit of economic growth, an expanding population will create a dangerous disadvantage.

Even if these trends simply change the nature of work, rather than reducing the overall number of jobs, the demands on education systems and worker retraining programs will be much more expensive in countries with larger populations. Finally, everyone—and every nation—sometimes needs to express frustration. Here, democracies have an important advantage over authoritarian states by allowing space for protest and other demonstrations of public anger. Protesters in states with free speech, free media, and freedom of assembly are less likely to face police or soldiers ready to use live ammunition, making it less likely that a small local protest will become a large national riot. This pressure valve allows a nation to absorb shock while minimizing the risk of a broader upheaval.

TWELVE COUNTRIES

With the need for resilience in mind, we turn to twelve of the world's largest and most important developing countries: China, India, Indonesia, Russia, Turkey, Brazil, Mexico, Venezuela, Nigeria, Saudi Arabia, Egypt, and South Africa. Begin with trust in government and its institutions. According to the 2017 Edelman Trust Barometer, trust in government is highest among the large Asian markets: China, India, and Indonesia. It's certainly possible that will change over time as public expectation of ever higher standards of living are dashed, but the evidence says that these countries have the advantage of starting from a higher base of confidence. Brazil and Mexico earn middle-of-the-pack scores, which is remarkable given the public scandals that have dominated local news in those countries in recent years. South Africa and Turkey score lower. Despite the continuing popularity of President Vladimir Putin, Russia scores very poorly, an ominous sign for what his successors might expect.[23]

Beyond this study, we can say that Saudi trust in government is based largely on the state's ability to employ two-thirds of the working-age population in government jobs.[24] In sharply polarized Venezuela, attitudes toward government are shaped almost entirely by allegiance (or lack thereof) to the ruling party. In Nigeria, split evenly between Christians and Muslims of the north, confidence in government and its institutions is shaped largely by the identity of the president.

The force most likely to further undermine confidence in government is the pace and scale of technological change in the workplace. There are two factors to consider. The first is vulnerability to automation and its disruptive effects. The second is the state's capacity to respond to it. Think of it like this: Is your home built on a fault line, and is it strong enough to withstand an earthquake?[25] The nature of their economies and the limitations of their politics make India, Indonesia, Russia, Nigeria, Saudi Arabia, Egypt, and South Africa especially vulnerable. Oil exporter Venezuela is less likely to automate. Mexico, Brazil, and China have more capacity than the rest to respond to the changes that automation will bring.

To measure demographic vulnerability, look to the share of a given population under the age of twenty-four and to national incomes per capita. Countries with large populations of young people need more jobs, and per capita income helps us account for big differences in size of the countries in question. According to statistics provided by the International Monetary Fund (IMF) and United Nations Development Programme (UNDP), the most vulnerable countries are Nigeria, Egypt, Venezuela, India, Indonesia, and South Africa. Mexico, Russia, Turkey, Brazil, and especially China are less vulnerable. South Africa, Brazil, Mexico, Saudi Arabia, China, Nigeria, and India suffer from the highest levels of income inequality. Indonesia, Russia, Turkey, Argentina, and Venezuela are less vulnerable. Egypt is the least vulnerable in this category.

But beyond these broad comparisons, we need a much closer look at the unique pressures squeezing each of these twelve countries. The next chapter will provide one.

CHAPTER 3

FAULT LINES

We learn geology the morning after the earthquake.

—RALPH WALDO EMERSON

S outh Africa, Nigeria, Egypt, Saudi Arabia, Brazil, Mexico, Venezuela, Turkey, Russia, Indonesia, India, and China have all undergone enormous changes over the past twenty-five years. Each has its strengths and vulnerabilities. Together, these countries contain well over half the people on earth and an even higher percentage of the world's youth. Their fate will determine the future of the entire twenty-first-century global economy.

Begin in sub-Saharan Africa, a region with fast-growing cities and economies, swelling populations of young people, weak political systems, underdeveloped infrastructure, and long histories of religious, sectarian, and tribal conflict.

SOUTH AFRICA

In recent years, student rage has taken center stage in South Africa. Cameras beam images of flying rocks, rubber bullets, riot gear, pepper spray, stun grenades, and flames across the country and around the world. This is a nation where young people understand the past very differently than their parents and have much deeper fears for the future. Bubbling beneath the surface of these protests is the fear that their country has no place for them, that their degrees won't earn them a chance at a better life, and that government doesn't care. There are nearly 20 million South Africans between the ages of fifteen and thirty-five, and just 6.2 million of them have jobs.[1]

How did this happen? From 2004 to 2008, a moment of high growth across the emerging-market world, high prices for the gold, platinum, diamonds, and coal that the country produces in abundance, along with the surge in state spending that the commodity boom enabled, helped South Africa grow by a robust 4.8 percent. From 2009 to 2013, as both rich and poor countries struggled to recover from a global economic slowdown, growth tumbled to just 1.9 percent.

Things have gotten worse. From 2014 to 2016, the figure fell to 1.1 percent, and the average number of violent protests climbed from 21 per year during the good times (2004–2008) to 164 per year in recent years (2014–2016). Youth unemployment is double the rate for adults, and it's nearly four times higher for black youth (40 percent) than for white youth (11 percent).

Those numbers translate fear and frustration into us vs. them.[2] "Them" can be the governing elite or the police or white people or foreign investors or an older generation of South Africans who don't understand the younger generation. Or it can be unwelcome foreign workers from places like Somalia, Nigeria, or Zimbabwe, particularly in parts of the country where poverty and joblessness are especially high. Guest workers have been the victims of attacks many times over many years.

The peaceful end of apartheid and the transition to genuine democracy in South Africa in the early 1990s stands among the greatest human achievements of the twentieth century. This success was a reflection of the wisdom of Nelson Mandela and the courage of South Africa's people. But a quarter century later, this remains one of the most unequal societies in the world. Despite hopes for rapid development with broadly shared benefits after apartheid fell, per capita income stands at just $5,200, and much of the country's wealth remains in white hands or with the black political and business elite. Poverty and joblessness remain chronic problems, particularly for young people, boosting what is already one of the highest crime rates on earth. World Bank statistics show that inequality has increased since the turn of the century.

Under former presidents Nelson Mandela and Thabo Mbeki, the state spent a lot of money to create opportunities for people who needed them most, but unemployment has risen above 25 percent during the scandal-plagued presidency of Jacob Zuma. Only about 30 percent of South African households qualify as middle income. A generation ago, many expected

South Africa to lead sub-Saharan Africa toward a development model that reduced inequality. That hasn't happened, and the country is now headed in the wrong direction.

Some of South Africa's weakness comes from falling global demand for the commodities it exports, reducing the money that government can invest. But some of these failures flow from the physical legacy of apartheid, the townships and under-developed rural areas that continue to separate poor people from the chance to learn and work. Drive the highways that separate South African cities from the dusty, sprawling townships, and you'll see people of every description, most unable to afford the transportation that might take them to a job, trudging along the side of the road.

Some of it comes down to chronic corruption and poor leadership from the African National Congress (ANC), which has ruled in coalition with the Congress of South African Trade Unions and South African Communist Party since apartheid's end without a serious electoral challenge. That's now changing, as both the moderate Democratic Alliance, which has won control of many local governments in recent years, and the Economic Freedom Fighters, a party of young people with a talent for political theater, inspired by Cuba's Fidel Castro and Venezuela's Hugo Chávez, capitalize on growing impatience and frustration with the ANC. The ruling party itself is increasingly divided. There is a globalist old guard that remains committed to private-sector-driven growth and openness to foreign investment. There is also an increasingly populist wing, still loyal to Zuma, that accuses foreigners of stealing South Africa's resources and white South Africans of continuing to control more than their fair share of the country's land and wealth.

Today, no South African under the age of thirty is old enough to remember apartheid. For many of these young people, the ANC is not the party of liberation but of power and privilege. They see globalization not as a source of personal empowerment, a rising tide that lifts all boats, but as a tool that foreigners use to steal South Africa's natural wealth. In that sense, they have more in common with Steve Bannon than with Nelson Mandela.

Younger people are voting in smaller numbers than in the past, a sign of cynicism toward the entire political class, but the number of campus protests is on the rise. There's a government plan to subsidize youth wages to encourage employers to hire young people, but the country's powerful trade unions oppose the subsidy on behalf of their members and will use their political influence to prevent it from becoming permanent.

South Africa is also especially vulnerable to the disruptive effects of automation of the workplace, because unemployment is already extraordinarily high, leaving much of its surging population of young people without even the most basic job skills. The South African government doesn't have the money to address that problem by upgrading primary, secondary, and higher education or to invest in research and development of new technologies at home. What is the future for South Africa's growing youth population? What happens when their frustration reaches a tipping point? And how will the ruling African National Congress—once the beating heart of resistance to apartheid-era oppression—respond when its dominance of South African politics is no longer assured?

We'll find out soon. That day is coming sooner than many think.

NIGERIA

Nigeria is profoundly divided too. Christian farmers and Muslims herders have fought battles that have killed hundreds. Muslim militants in the country's north have killed thousands. Militia groups in the southern Niger Delta region have attacked state officials, police, foreigners, and foreign companies that they accuse of stealing the region's oil wealth. It's unusual in this country to see a large-scale urban protest against inequality and government corruption. Yet, in 2017, on one cloudy February afternoon in Lagos, the country's commercial hub, hundreds of protesters stopped traffic and serenaded local police with chants of "Government of the rich, for the rich, making rules for the poor" against a backdrop of music from the late Afrobeat icon and political dissident Fela Kuti.[3]

With more than 180 million people, Nigeria is Africa's most populous country and its largest economy. It's also an increasingly unequal society. A 2017 study published by Oxfam and Development Finance International put Nigeria dead last on its list of 152 countries ranked by "commitment to reducing inequality." The report labels Nigeria's spending on public health and education as "shamefully low" and notes that "Nigeria's richest man earns 8,000 times more in one day than a poor Nigerian will spend on basic needs in a year."

The problem is getting worse. Nigeria's economy has grown at a strong pace in recent years, but the study notes that it is one of the few countries where the number of people living in poverty has increased—from 69 million in 2004 to 112 million in 2010—over the past generation.[4] That's a rise of nearly 70 percent, and it means that more than 65 percent of the population is poor. "The number of millionaires increased by 44 percent during the same period," according to the study, drawing a clear boundary between globalization's winners and losers.[5] The country's per capita income is $2,200.

Nigeria has a population divided almost evenly between Christians in the country's southern states and the underdeveloped Muslim-dominated north. To build confidence and a shared stake in the country's future as democracy took hold in 1999, leaders of the Muslim north and Christian south struck an informal deal for a regional rotation of the country's presidency. Yet southerners have held the job for thirteen of nineteen years since. The first northern president, Umaru Yar'Adua, died in 2010 after just three years in office and was replaced by his southern vice president. The second, current President Muhammadu Buhari, has been ill for much of his term. Failure to share power as promised hasn't created a crisis yet, and the first peaceful transition of power from a defeated incumbent to his challenger in 2015 offered a positive sign for the country's cohesion.

But unresolved north-south tensions will become a much larger problem if economic growth slows sharply or if unemployment spikes. That's exactly what's begun to happen.

The lower price of oil, which accounts for more than 90 percent of Nigeria's export revenue, has weighed heavily on economic growth in this OPEC member country, reducing the government's ability to spend on education, better infrastructure, and other attempts to reduce poverty, particularly in the northern states. The percentage of northern children in school is half the percentage in the south, as money from the country's oil industry and the service sector in Nigeria's largest cities, both of which are centered in the south, is not shared with northern states. Boko Haram, an Islamist militant group based in the country's northeast that has killed more than 15,000 people and pushed more than 2 million from their homes, makes matters worse by making a poor region poorer. In the far south, militants in the oil-producing region of the Niger Delta continue to plague production.

Nigeria, like Saudi Arabia, Russia, Venezuela, and others, needs to diversify its economy away from heavy dependence on oil exports, but its inequality will work against this process because, as the elite within developing countries amass wealth, they may lose the incentive to invest in the country's future. The introduction of automation into the country's manufacturing and artificial intelligence into its service sector will create turmoil in the country's overcrowded cities mainly because, as in South Africa, the country's education system is ill-equipped to prepare a fast-expanding population of young people for twenty-first-century jobs. The World Bank estimates that automation and machine learning will put 65 percent of all current jobs in Nigeria at risk. This may be the factor that finally tips Nigeria toward real turmoil.

EGYPT

"We want to eat!" It's the simplest of protest slogans. In March 2017, bread riots erupted in a number of Egyptian cities as thousands of angry people blocked off busy streets and surrounded state-run bakeries to vent their fury at a government decision to reduce the number of subsidized bread loaves that each family was allowed to buy. Egyptians have many reasons to be angry with their government, but none is more basic than this.

Inequality is growing in Egypt. Nearly 30 percent of the country's 90 million people live in poverty, the highest level since the turn of the century. Its per capita income is less than $3,500, and fallout from the Arab Spring continues. The problems that helped create that 2011 uprising—particularly public anger that the vast majority of Egypt's people have never benefited from higher economic growth and that government exercised unchecked power over people's lives—remain unresolved following the military's recapture of government in 2014.

President Abdel Fattah al-Sisi has tightened his grip by isolating both the moderate and more radicalized supporters of Egypt's Muslim Brotherhood. Yet resistance is growing. Terrorist attacks in Egypt have taken a human and economic toll, particularly on the important tourism sector, and the Egyptian government was forced to declare a three-month state of emergency in 2017 following attacks on Egyptian Christians.[6] The resulting government crackdown on Sisi's political challengers has discouraged both domestic and foreign investment in the country's future. Financial help from Saudi Arabia and other Persian Gulf states has slowed sharply as lower oil prices force these countries to spend their money more carefully. Demands from the International Monetary Fund that Egypt allow a devaluation of its currency have pushed prices higher across the country, hitting the poor especially hard. Complicating matters further, the Egyptian military, anxious to protect political stability and its economic privileges, can veto the civilian government's attempts to introduce reforms that might help Egypt solve some of its lasting problems.

But this country's greatest challenge will come from its exploding population, which has grown from 66 million in 2000 to more than 90 million today. It is projected to reach 120 million by 2030 and 150 million by 2050.[7] Population growth and urban sprawl leave less room for agriculture, exacerbating alarming shortages of food and water in a country that is already the world's largest importer of wheat. There have been protests over rising prices for food and fuel, as in November 2016, when the government devalued Egypt's currency and cut fuel subsidies to try to get its financial house in order, and again in March 2017, when it took that extraordinary step of cutting bread subsidies.[8]

More than half of Egypt's population is under twenty-five.

Some 750,000 Egyptians graduate college each year, but few have the skills needed to succeed in the current workforce.[9] Some young people with little hope for a better life will blame their government. Others will blame the IMF, an institution closely identified with globalism, which insists on state spending cuts in exchange for its loans. Near-term, large-scale automation is unlikely in Egypt, because a government that can't supply bread is unlikely to spend on development of new technologies or on programs to train workers how to use them. The inability to innovate will only leave Egypt that much further behind, and more people with fewer opportunities will surely need someone to blame.

SAUDI ARABIA

In May 2012, a group of men serving as religious police, known in Saudi Arabia as the Commission for the Promotion of Virtue and Prevention of Vice, approached a young woman in a shopping mall. They told her that since she was wearing polish on her fingernails, she would have to leave. "I'm staying, and I want to know what you're going to do about it," the young woman replied. She recorded the encounter on her phone and posted the resulting video on YouTube, where more than a million people saw it within days of the incident. The battle between us and them, between those who want greater personal freedom in Saudi Arabia and those who believe these values are foreign and will contaminate the kingdom, played out vividly in the YouTube comments section with strong opinions, colorfully expressed, on both sides.[10] Not all young Saudis want a more open society. Many have become Twitter followers of some of the kingdom's most outspoken conservative clerics. In other words, some young Saudis have embraced globalism and others have not.

Five years later, a woman was arrested for posting a video of herself walking through the streets of a small Saudi village wearing a short skirt and sneakers. Twitter users posted evidence that Riyadh police had issued an arrest warrant that charged the young woman with "disrespecting and violating the teachings of Islam."[11] Nearly half of the country's 32 million people are under the age of twenty-five, but a close look at social media in the kingdom reveals that even the youngest Saudis are divided over questions of freedom and religious conformity. These tensions have existed for years, but they will run much higher if the Saudi government can't provide them jobs, income, or greater opportunities to live as they choose.

There is no country quite like Saudi Arabia. Its per capita income is above $20,000, more than five times higher than in Egypt and nine times higher than in Nigeria, but that's only because it's a much smaller country that sits on a lot of oil. It has a large and growing population of young people, but two-thirds of the workforce is employed by the government, many of them in undemanding positions created to make work rather than to fuel growth. Physical labor is virtually always performed by foreigners from poor countries hoping to send money home. Expats and foreign guest workers with no path to citizenship make up nearly a third of Saudi Arabia's population of 32 million and about 75 percent of the private-sector workforce, according to the IMF.

The Saudi economy doesn't depend for growth on productive workers or technological innovation. The state doesn't depend for revenue on taxes paid by citizens. For decades, the answer to every question has been crude oil, which accounts for nearly 90 percent of total exports and more than 90 percent of the government's budget revenue. That's where the money comes from to pay all those government workers with so little to do.

But the world's energy markets are undergoing revolutionary change. New technologies are helping oil companies find energy deposits they would not have found ten years ago and extract the oil from new places, and in new ways, that were recently impossible. The result is that known global reserves of crude oil are now almost 2.5 times higher than in 1980, and abundant available supply ensures that prices won't anytime soon recover to the peak they reached in 2014, if ever.[12] Add the fact that economies around the world will rely more over time on a fuel mix that's less dependent on oil, and the Saudis will find themselves without the seemingly endless inflow of petrodollars that they've enjoyed for decades. That won't happen tomorrow or the day after, because the Saudis still have plenty of cash on hand. But the day of reckoning is coming, the impact will be permanent, and the Saudi leadership knows it.

That's why King Salman has launched the Vision 2030 project, an enormously ambitious plan, directed by his enormously ambitious son, to enact the economic, technological, and social changes needed to modernize the Saudi economy and create millions of good jobs for young Saudis. Bring women into the workforce by allowing them to drive. End harassment of young people by the religious police. Persuade citizens that the state will wage war on corruption, even if it's committed by members of the royal family. Change society to change the economy. Will it work? Unlike countries such as South Africa, Nigeria, and Egypt, the Saudi government has money to spend on education. About 90 percent of Saudi children are now in school, and women outnumber men among university graduates. This is the foundation that makes Vision 2030 possible.

But there are reasons for doubt, despite the talent and sincerity of the man leading the project, Crown Prince Mohammad bin Salman. Changing the Saudi economy means changing Saudi society, by creating a national work ethic in a country that has never had one—and by welcoming women not just into the classroom but into the workforce in much larger numbers, even if they don't all dress in ways that satisfy religious conservatives. It's one thing to change the law, another to abolish long-observed traditions. King Salman has imposed austerity measures for the sake of a more sustainable economic system. Subsidies have been reduced, raising the prices that citizens pay for water, electricity, and fuel. Free health care and free education could be eliminated next. It's a short-term gamble that the king hopes will build a more sustainable long-term strategy. But the larger question is how this country will create the jobs its rising population of young people will need.

And what happens if the Saudi public can no longer be satisfied, if ambitious members of the royal family use public anger to boost their own standing within the ruling elite, creating discord in the process? In the search for a "them" to rally "us," the Saudis are likely to pick more fights with regional rival Iran, creating more frustration and anger inside the kingdom and across the region. Many Saudi young people, meanwhile, will continue to push for a new way of life.

BRAZIL

Brazil is the classic example of a country where government has become a victim of its own success. The country's middle class grew from about 35 percent of the population when the Workers Party government came to power in 2003 to nearly 60 percent by 2013. That's a major leap forward for tens of millions of people. It has less to do with well-diversified trade—Brazil's economy is much less open than other major emerging markets—than with the resource-rich country's ability to ship commodities to China and its government's willingness to redirect wealth toward people who had long been excluded via programs like Fome Zero (Zero Hunger) and Bolsa Familia (Family Grant) that have helped poor people afford food, gain access to water, borrow money, vaccinate children, and send them to school.

Yet enormous numbers of people who have been lifted from poverty, and those already in the middle class, now demand much better government—and their expectations have been heightened at an especially difficult moment for Brazil. In recent years, prices of Brazil's commodity exports have fallen sharply. Brazil's currency lost one-third of its value in 2015. Government, companies, and consumers have accumulated mountains of debt. In a country mired in recession for the past several years, with a public infuriated by daily updates on the biggest political scandal in the nation's history, millions of Brazilians are fed up—with corruption, crime, a lack of good schools and quality health care, and gross government incompetence.[13] It's one thing for government to transfer large amounts of wealth to people who need it. It's another to provide them with the services that middle-class citizens expect. That requires large amounts of investment. Investment requires careful planning, intelligent policymaking, painful reform, and political compromise. All have been hard to come by in postboom Brazil.

Per capita income remains at just $8,700, and Brazil needs to spend much more on basic infrastructure—better roads, bridges, schools, hospitals, ports, and airports—if it is to escape the ongoing economic slowdown that threatens to reverse many of the Brazilian people's gains. Yet the slowing economy makes that more difficult every year, and the inability of politicians to sustain their popularity for very long makes tough-minded reform that much harder to impose. Anger is rising against an entire political establishment that has not found an effective response, and protests have reached historic heights. This is a country where the battle of us vs. them now pits citizens against the entire political and business elite.

MEXICO

Brazil's political and business scandals have grown so big that they've spilled over into a number of other countries. Odebrecht, an enormous Brazilian construction company and a key player in the Lava Jato scandal, was accused in 2017 of bribing officials in Mexico in exchange for big state contracts. This was just the latest stain on the presidency of Enrique Peña Nieto, who was elected in 2012 with an approval rating of 54 percent and a mandate to undertake ambitious reforms, including a historic opening of the oil industry that promises to bring large amounts of foreign investment over time to modernize the oil sector. He achieved that goal, but it will be many years before Mexico sees substantial return.

So much has gone wrong. The kidnap and murder of forty-three students in the southern Mexican state of Guerrero in September 2014—a landmark case that produced accusations against criminal gangs, local police, federal police, and even the army—provoked nationwide protests in October 2014 and again in August 2015. The story continues to haunt the country, because it suggests to many people that the rule of law remains arbitrary and that the country's political culture is hopelessly corrupt. Add a financial scandal involving the president's wife, the state's suspicious inability to keep drug kingpin Joaquín "El Chapo" Guzmán behind bars, a weaker currency, and the decision to withdraw a popular gasoline subsidy, and Peña Nieto's popularity had fallen to 17 percent by 2017.

In Mexico, citizens are increasingly frustrated with corruption at all levels of government, rising inflation, mediocre growth for the past generation, and a worsening security situation. Mexico has not experienced the sudden surge in income and expectations that we've seen in Brazil and some other emerging markets. In fact, the country's real minimum wage hasn't grown in twenty years, and the rate of poverty hasn't much changed in twenty-five, leaving few Mexicans with confidence that tomorrow's living standards will be better than yesterday's. A surge in U.S. oil production is bad news for a country that still sends more than 70 percent of its oil exports to the United States. This is another developing country that badly needs revenue for investment: Mexico ranks thirtieth of thirty-five OECD countries in education spending and thirty-second in health care spending.

This is an interesting moment for Mexico. At a time when the center-right is making a comeback across much of Latin America, public anger in Mexico, fueled by new attacks from Donald Trump, may boost the popularity of the country's most talented populist—just in time for a presidential election in 2018. Andrés Manuel López Obrador hopes to capitalize on frustration with corruption and fear of both criminal gangs and their enablers within the police to launch a full electoral assault on the current government. The rest of the political establishment fears that López Obrador will try to please voters by reversing policies designed to provide long-term economic gains, like opening the country's energy sector to foreign investment, and that he'll open investigations that might throw many of the country's current leaders in jail. As in Brazil, the risk is that fed-up voters will treat the entire political class as "them," creating an opportunity for a candidate promising to punish the country's elite and protect its interests against assaults from the giant neighbor to the north and its bellicose president.

Finally, Mexico is a country where automation will have a big effect. Nearly two-thirds of jobs in advanced manufacturing of automobiles, aerospace products, and plastics can be automatized. That's good news for companies and shareholders, but it's bad news for the estimated 5 million workers who will be displaced.[14] Add that disruption to the country's middle class and the impact it will have on wealth inequality, and this will be a volatile and dangerous moment in Mexico's history.

VENEZUELA

There are many types of shortages. In Venezuela, water was in such short supply by 2016 that citizens added to their meager rations by stealing water from swimming pools and tanker trucks. Electricity shortages forced the government to order public offices to open just two days a week. Power cuts and rolling blackouts became part of daily life. Aspirin disappeared off store shelves. Supermarkets closed because they had nothing to sell. In April 2016, Empresas Polar, Venezuela's largest private company and producer of 80 percent of all beer consumed in the country, suspended production. "Let them drink water," government officials might have said, if there had been any water.

Venezuela is blessed (or cursed) with the world's largest oil reserves. Yet it has suffered much higher levels of unrest in recent years than any other Latin American country. Former President Hugo Chávez, an iconic populist firebrand, invested in improving the lives of poor people long ignored by Venezuela's political class. State spending cut the country's poverty rate nearly in half during his presidency, from 49 percent in 1999 to just 29 percent in 2012. Inequality was sharply reduced. Record high oil prices helped Chávez introduce the so-called *misiones*, which provided the poor with subsidized food, basic goods, housing, and health care. His popularity allowed him to consolidate power at the expense of the country's democracy and to create all sorts of long-term economic problems.

In 2013, Chávez died. In late 2014, oil prices fell by almost half. A country that imports virtually everything except crude oil quickly faced serious (and lasting) shortages of food, water, and other basic goods. Nicolás Maduro, Chávez's hapless successor, has struggled to beat back demands for political change. Venezuela's economy has been in deep recession for many years. Scarce goods, an overvalued exchange rate, and the government's attempt to manage its debt by printing way too much money have sent price inflation skyrocketing. Product shortages will get worse as the government vows to spend less on imports to ensure it can continue to avoid default on sovereign debt.

The black market has threatened to wreck what's left of the consumer economy as state-imposed price controls create opportunities for Venezuelans to make more money buying state-subsidized goods and reselling them at higher prices, or smuggling them over the border into Colombia, than they can by working. Extreme poverty has nearly doubled during this crisis, from about a quarter of the country's population to more than half, reversing the gains made under Chávez. Venezuela's cities have some of the highest rates of violent crime in the world. Many young people with enough money are leaving the country.

Like Chávez, Maduro uses the ruling party's control of the country's courts to keep the opposition from power. When opposition candidates won a majority of seats in the national assembly in December 2015, a supreme court packed with Maduro loyalists dissolved the assembly. Street demonstrations have turned violent, and more than one hundred citizens have been killed. Chávez and Maduro have ensured that loyal allies command Venezuela's military. That loyalty will continue—perhaps until the order is given to fire on Venezuelan men, women, and children.

Venezuela's economy will not improve under the current system, and regime change is increasingly likely. It remains unclear, as of this writing, when and how the end will come—and how many will die in the process. It will take years for even the most capable opposition-led government to correct the distortions that Chávez and Maduro have imposed on Venezuela's economy, particularly if they try to do it without imposing excruciating economic pain on those that Chávez lifted from poverty. All these changes must come at a time when diversifying the country's economy away from deep dependence on oil exports has never seemed further out of reach.

TURKEY

Turkey has faced plenty of unrest of its own. Recep Tayyip Erdogan and his Justice and Development Party deserve enormous credit for making Turkey one of the world's most exciting economic success stories of the first decade of the new century. Past governments had simply reinforced the power of elites in the country's largest cities: Istanbul, Ankara, and Izmir. Wealth remained in the hands of the small number of families who dominated Turkish business. Traditions institutionalized by Mustafa Kemal Ataturk, modern Turkey's founding father, ensured strict adherence to secularism in the nation's political life and an orientation toward Europe as a model for political and social development. Turkey's military has historically served as protector of these principles. Erdogan's innovation was to empower citizens and small businesses across the country's Anatolian heartland to join in the political and economic life of their country. He challenged secular dominance of government to allow Turks with conservative social values a greater role in the country's development. Per capita income tripled during the first decade of his political dominance, and Turkey became a more influential actor on the global stage.

Yet Erdogan let success go to his head, and Turkey's political system has not yet proved strong enough to restrain him. As he works to remain in power, he pushes economic policies that he believes will help in the short run but which are certain to deepen long-term problems. Prevented by the rules of his party from continuing as prime minister, he won election as president in 2014 and proposed a referendum that would allow a rewrite of Turkey's constitution to give the presidency much more power. He beat back media criticism by putting journalists in jail. When criticism moved to social media, he tried to ban Twitter.

Well aware that Turkey has a history of military coups, he used warnings of conspiracy to periodically purge the army's ranks. In July 2016, some parts of the army finally did try to see him off, but Erdogan eluded capture and declared a state of emergency that gave him extraordinary powers to imprison large numbers of enemies, real and imagined, and to further tighten his control of courts, the bureaucracy, the police, and the army. His supporters, many of them empowered and embold-ened by his success in increasing the heartland's influence in the life of the country, lifted him to a narrow referendum victory in 2017.*[15] For these citizens, crisis can legitimize a tough authori-tarian response.

Yet Turkey's problems continue to mount. On the one hand, the percentage of those living in poverty has been dramatically reduced—from more than 30 percent in 2002 to just 1.6 percent in 2014. However, among thirty-five OECD countries, only Mexico has greater income inequality than Turkey. Erdogan is also endangered by the economic expectations created by earlier success. In 2012, his party promised that per capita income would climb to $25,000 by 2023. In 2016, it remained just above $10,700. He continues to amass power, but election results tell

---

*Critics charge that the vote was rigged.

us there are a significant number of people in his country who oppose his plans to expand it indefinitely.

At the same time, his country's economy remains stuck in low gear, capping even the gains made by his supporters in years past. Erdogan's pressure to keep interest rates low to protect growth and his popularity, along with his reluctance to enact painful reforms that will strengthen the country over the long term, leave Turkey unusually vulnerable to external economic shocks. And as in other developing countries, the government has not kept pace with the need to spend more on urban infrastructure as more and more young Turks move to the country's largest cities with hopes for a better life.

In response to tough times and heightened criticism, Erdogan has proved to be a master of the politics of us vs. them. Beyond political opponents, journalists, and Kurds, he has played to the grievances of many of his supporters—particularly conservative Muslims and hard-core nationalists—by picking colorful fights with European governments. During the referendum, he used the word "Nazi" more than once to describe both German and Dutch officials and their actions. But his most intense fights are with rivals at home, including at times members of his own party, whom he accuses of betraying the country and its president. He has accused journalists who criticize him of abetting terrorism. In the process, Erdogan has further polarized an already divided country. He will continue to push for more power. Those who fear him will continue to push back. There will be more confrontations in Turkey's streets.

RUSSIA

In Russia, we find another smart, charismatic leader who could once claim credit for a major surge in living standards—one supported, as in Venezuela, by historically high oil prices. After the political and economic chaos of the first post-Soviet decade, capped with a financial crisis in 1998, per capita income tripled during the first decade of Vladimir Putin's consolidation of power (2000–2010). The share of Russians living below the national poverty line fell from 29 percent in 2000 to just 10.7 percent in 2012. His government built state-controlled wealth funds, with vast sums generated by the export of oil, gas, metals, and minerals, as insurance against future economic turmoil.

But thanks mainly to the steep drop in oil prices since 2014, Russia's per capita income remains stuck below $9,000 per year, less than in former satellites like the Czech Republic ($18,286), Slovakia ($16,499), Hungary ($12,778), and Poland ($12,316) that have joined the European Union. Oil now accounts for less than half of Russian government revenue only because the price has fallen sharply. State-controlled wealth funds have lost much of their cash as Putin invests in Russia's military muscle and tries to protect entitlements for the country's most vulnerable. Western sanctions haven't helped.

In response to tougher times, state officials have stopped increasing pensions in line with inflation. They have halted most public-sector wage increases in a country where one-third of citizens work for the state or for state-owned companies. They have slashed financial support for regional governments, even as seventy-seven of Russia's eighty-three regions run deficits and amass debt. Poverty, already on the rise in recent years, will continue climbing, particularly for pensioners and those who live far from the largest cities, the most reliable of Putin's supporters. Well-educated Russians are leaving the country in search of better prospects. Russia's life expectancy ranks 153rd in the world.

The gap between rich and poor is now wider in Russia than in all but four of thirty-five OECD countries, though the growth of Russia's black market mitigates the damage. In 2014, at a time when oil still sold at well above $100 per barrel, Russia's shadow economy already amounted to an estimated 40 percent of GDP, while 24 percent of the country's wealth was held offshore. There's no reason to believe that either statistic has improved since then.

For now, the greatest source of public anger at Russia's government is the corruption that continues to drive the protests described in the last chapter. State dominance of Russian media, his tough-guy image, and his ability to deflect blame for corruption and a weakening economy onto subordinates have helped Putin continue to defy political gravity. Yet questions remain. Without an unlikely lasting surge in oil prices, what force can reverse the steady decline of Russia's economy and living standards? How will Russians respond to the repression of political dissent when trouble becomes commonplace in parts of the country where support for Putin remains high? What foreign policy gambles might Putin take to divert public attention from Russia's decline?

Remember that Levada Center poll from the last chapter? More than half of Russians surveyed in 2017 said they were tired of waiting for Putin to improve their lives. How long can he escape blame if things don't improve? In the past, many Russians have been reluctant to challenge a government that pays their salaries or those of a family member. How long will that reluctance last as wages stagnate and living standards fall? Protests have already expanded well beyond Russia's largest cities. How long before public frustration becomes a major political challenge for the Russian government? Putin remains broadly popular, protesters can be punished, there are no credible challengers available to voters, and Russia still has lots of money for rainy days. Yet this country is headed slowly but steadily in a bad direction, and it's not clear what force might finally turn things around.

INDONESIA

One warm morning in December 2016, 200,000 Indonesian Muslims descended on Jakarta, the country's capital, to demand that Basuki Tjahaja Purnama be thrown in jail. According to the mob, he had insulted Islam by publicly quoting a verse from the Koran with an interpretation they didn't like. The crowd's real motive? This ethnic Chinese Christian governor of Jakarta province, better known as Ahok, was locked in a close battle for reelection, and Muslim populists wanted to see him lose. "Jail Ahok. The law must be fair," read the banners.[16]

Though Indonesia is officially a secular country, religious

freedom and diversity remain enshrined in the country's constitution, and Ahok remains a friend and ally of Indonesia's reformist president, a court convicted him of "blasphemy" in May 2017 and sentenced him to two years in prison. This is the latest sign that the politics of us vs. them is now playing a larger role in the life of the world's most populous majority-Muslim country, as radical Islam, populism, and nationalism expand their political appeal.

Indonesia is home to an estimated 260 million people. It's a poor country, with per capita income of just $3,600. Beyond large-scale poverty, Indonesia is burdened with a large gap between rich and poor, one that has grown much wider since the East Asian financial crisis twenty years ago. That's one of the most important reasons that Indonesians elected the former reformist governor of Jakarta province, Joko Widodo, as their president in 2014. Jokowi, as he's widely known, is the country's first president to come from outside Indonesia's traditional elite, and he has attacked inequality through a sharp increase in state spending on the country's ramshackle infrastructure, as well as its education and health care systems.

But Indonesia is yet another developing country where politicians and the business elite eat at the same table and corruption remains endemic. So far, the wealthy and well connected who oppose reform continue to target Jokowi's plans rather than the popular president himself. That will change if failure to deliver higher living standards leaves Jokowi vulnerable. There is also a geographical divide within the country. About 120 million of the country's 260 million people live far from major cities on Indonesia's more than 17,000 underdeveloped smaller islands, and they have a lot of catching up to do. The private sector sees little profit opportunity in investing in these islands, and the state lacks the money to make up the difference, because this is a country where government isn't good at collecting taxes.

Jokowi presses on. The number of Indonesians over age fifteen grew by more than 3 million between 2014 and 2015, while the number of jobs grew by just 200,000.[17] The poor can expect more cash transfers and education subsidies to give them a better chance at middle-class life. The rich can expect higher taxes. Yet Indonesia's vast population (the world's fourth largest), its youth bulge (half the country is under twenty-eight), its urban-rural divide, and the very large number of poorly educated, low-skilled workers make the country especially vulnerable to the coming revolution in the automation of manufacturing. If Jokowi can't raise enough revenue and pass legislation to invest much more in better roads, better schools, and more electricity beyond Java, young Indonesians will never develop the skills they need to compete in a digital-age East Asian economy. The country's divides will grow, its reform movement will be discredited, and tens of millions of Indonesians will slide back into poverty.

The elite will build more gated communities and private schools. The poor will turn to local schools and organizations that promote an Indonesian brand of Sunni Islam that rejects the government's traditional "unity in diversity" message of tolerance, an idea that has helped keep the peace for many years in a country with large ethnic and religious minorities. Given their numbers, an aggrieved underclass might then use the ballot box to elect leaders who promise to use any means necessary to right what they believe is wrong. That's not difficult to imagine in a country where we already see Islamist parties promote Muslim dominance and nationalist parties demand loyalty to patriotic values as they define them.

INDIA

One evening in September 2017, Gauri Lankesh, an Indian journalist with a famously satirical sense of humor, returned home after a long day at work. A few steps from her front door, she was shot dead by an unknown drive-by assailant. As news spread, speculation about a motive began and protests erupted in cities across the country. On one side were friends and allies of Lankesh, who claimed she was murdered by Hindu nationalists and their allies in government who wanted her punished for her reports on their brutality. On the other were politicians of the ruling Bharatiya Janata Party (BJP) and their allies, who insisted the motive was unknown and that government critics were exploiting her death for political gain.[18]

Seven decades after India's independence and partition from Muslim Pakistan, religion remains a focal point of the politics of us vs. them. It's frightening enough that there are still religiously motivated murders in this profoundly diverse country and that mob violence continues against Muslims accused of stealing, selling, or eating cows, which are sacred to many conservative Hindus. It's more alarming that political officials of the ruling BJP often fan these flames, including by calling journalists who criticize Hindu nationalism "sickular" and "presstitutes."[19]

With per capita income of just $1,723, fast-growing India remains the poorest of these twelve countries. A program of economic liberalization that began in the 1980s, accelerated with a debt crisis in 1991 and which continues today under reformist Prime Minister Narendra Modi, has sharply accelerated India's economic growth, but the ongoing (partial) dismantling of the labyrinthine socialist bureaucracy that makes growth acceleration possible has exacerbated income inequality.

The good news for India is that income inequality there is less severe than in fellow BRICS countries Brazil, Russia, China, and South Africa. The bad news: That's mainly because a much larger percentage of Indians are dirt poor. About 600 million of the country's more than one billion people get by on near-subsistence levels of farming, informal village-level jobs, and off-the-books, low-end manufacturing. A study published in 2017 by French economists Lucas Chancel and Thomas Piketty found that inequality in India and the share of national income that goes to the top 1 percent of wage earners are higher than at any point since Indians began paying income tax in 1922.[20] The days of the so-called Hindu rate of growth—the tepid expansions produced by India's state-dominated economy from independence in 1947 until the 1980s—appear to be gone. But the slow opening of India's economy, the expansion of its service sector, and its growing consumer class have so far benefited only a small percentage of the country's workforce.

Under Modi's leadership, India has become the fastest-growing large economy in the world, and near the top of his list of reform plans is a surge in investment in India's famously rusty infrastructure. Yet the country's needs are enormous. In 2012, before the BJP rose to power, a massive blackout highlighted the scale of one part of the problem by cutting electricity to 700 million people. The International Energy Agency estimated in 2015 that 240 million Indians live without any access to electricity. The government said it expects every household in India to have power by 2018, but the number of hours per day it lasts is another question.

As of 2014, 600 million people in India did not have a toilet inside their homes.[21] The government also said in 2015 that nearly 40 percent of the country's 5.4 million–kilometer road network remained unpaved.[22] In much of the country, the rail system is more than a hundred years old. In 2016, Finance Minister Arun Jaitley warned that the country needed $1.5 trillion in investment in roads, bridges, railways, ports, water sanitation, electricity grids, and other projects over the following decade to meet its basic infrastructure needs and maintain growth.[23]

Access to water is one of the country's biggest challenges and an important potential source of large-scale unrest. Nearly 76 million Indians still lack access to safe water, according to a 2016 estimate from WaterAid, a London-based nonprofit, and millions more drink water of very low quality.[24] Aquifers, which supply 85 percent of the country's water, are not being refilled. The water table is dropping, and birth rates are highest in the northern and western states where water is most in demand.

More than 600 million people in India make their living from agriculture, but nearly two-thirds of the country's farmland depends on rain for irrigation. Droughts can affect hundreds of millions of lives.[25] Climate change isn't helping; given the lack of water, a drop in rainfall totals during (increasingly erratic) seasonal monsoons can drive food prices higher, triggering riots by those unable to buy staples. This is already a big political issue in many of India's state elections.

Most important are the country's demographics. Within the next five years, India will surpass China to become the world's most populous country.[26] Unlike China and Russia, India has a fast-growing population of young people. Half the country is under the age of twenty-five, and 65 percent are under thirty-five. For now, that's good for economic growth. But even today there aren't enough jobs for the one million Indians who enter the workforce each month. Remember that, according to UN forecasts, automation and machine learning innovations in the workplace will put 69 percent of India's existing jobs at risk.

There are other challenges. Beyond the tensions, and sometimes bloodshed, that still plague relations between Hindu nationalists and a Muslim minority population of more than 100 million people, there are also still divisions defined by caste. Affirmative action policies that provide sought-after spots in the country's best institutions of higher learning and well-paid government jobs to lower-caste citizens stoke resentments among different groups—tensions that play out in local politics and sometimes in the streets. Over time, more groups will demand these privileges, and they'll vote for parliamentary candidates who promise to deliver them. It's difficult enough to govern a country in which thirty-five different languages are spoken by at least a million people each, with 22,000 distinct dialects, but fast-expanding access to social media will make protests easier to organize and harder to contain. Dynamic, ambitious India has defied warnings of impending doom for decades. But where will the jobs come from? How can India's government continue to meet rising expectations unless all these big structural problems are solved?

India has long been among the most protectionist of major emerging markets, its economic course set long ago by the Fabian Society socialism that founding father Jawaharlal Nehru absorbed during student years in Britain, and later by the determination of his daughter, Indira Gandhi, to protect state dominance of India's economy as a matter of national pride. This country's lead politicians have long been suspicious of "globalism" and the colonialist mind-set they see in its origins. Modi has opened some sectors of the economy to more foreign investment, but he and his BJP have also added a strong dose of Hindu nationalism to the mix. Globalization has created important opportunities for ambitious young Indians in recent decades, especially those with good command of English. But all those call centers, in Bangalore and other Indian cities, can soon be run by machines as artificial intelligence moves from the U.S. and European service sectors to poorer countries. Put it all together, and there's a serious risk that a new generation of Indian politicians will make names for themselves by pitting various versions of "us" against new versions of "them."

CHINA

Here is globalization's greatest success story.

China's rise can be measured in many ways, but the most impressive number is the 700 million people that state-led reform has lifted from poverty over the past four decades. In 1986, China's per capita GDP was $282. In 2016, it climbed above $8,100. The country's middle class represented 4 percent of the population in 2002 and 31 percent in 2013.[27] For the future, the Communist Party leadership says it can educate enough people, create enough jobs, stoke enough growth, and provide enough health care to boost 50 million more from the lowest income brackets by 2020. Despite predictions from many people over many years that a crash of China's economy is long overdue, the world's biggest emerging market and its aspirations remain aloft.

Yet, for a variety of reasons—all of them inevitable—the country's growth rates continue to slow, and its gains are under pressure. The 2008–2010 financial crisis in the West made clear to China's leaders that they must move more urgently to relieve the country's dependence for growth on the willingness of U.S. and European consumers to buy China's cheaply made manufactured goods. To lock in long-term economic stability, China needs to build and bolster its own middle class, one that can afford to buy much more of those factory-made consumer products. Success has pushed Chinese wages higher. But as pay rises, China loses the advantage that brought so many foreign companies to the country in the first place. Even Chinese companies have begun to move production to poorer countries, particularly in Southeast Asia, where labor is cheaper. Higher wages can't help you if you don't have a job.

Further, the problem of inequality has been growing for years. Even as hundreds of millions have climbed the ladder, the wealth gap has grown larger between the low-income population still trapped in the countryside, the new middle class, and the now superrich. The Gini coefficient has risen dramatically (from 0.27 in 1984 to 0.42 in 2010), but even that large jump probably doesn't capture the true scale of the problem. Statistical fraud at different levels of government undermines confidence in numbers we know are politically sensitive. We can be sure that the coastal regions of China are far richer than the interior and that, even by the standards of other developing countries, the gap between urban and rural wealth is large and growing.

Exacerbating inequality, if you live in Beijing, Shanghai, Guangzhou, or another city where incomes have risen quickly, you may have access to good schools. If you live outside the lead cities, you probably don't. Education will become an even more controversial subject over time, because the jobs of the future are much more likely to demand highly skilled, well-trained, and well-educated workers. And there's rising fear even in the best cities that surging prices, especially for housing, will drive out huge numbers of people.

Then there is the poisoned air and water, the bitter product of decades of surging economic growth. The statistics have become sadly familiar. China's Ministry of Environmental Protection has reported that two-thirds of China's groundwater and one-third of its surface water are unfit for human contact of any kind.[28] Toxins and garbage ensure that almost half the country's rivers fall into this category.[29] Estimates are that air pollution kills more than one million Chinese people per year.[30]

In addition, the country's social safety net remains a massive work in progress as China's population gets old faster than any-where else in the world, leaving fewer and fewer workers to produce the wealth needed to pay for care for the elderly. In 1980, the median age, the point that divides a population into two numerically equal halves, was 22.1 years in China and 30.1 years in the United States. A UN study has estimated that by 2050 the median age will be 40.6 in the United States and 46.3 in China. In the 1990s, China introduced a program called the Minimum Livelihood Guarantee Scheme, or Dibao, to provide small amounts of money to the poorest people. More recent projects designed to boost incomes for people living in the coun-tryside have reached hundreds of millions of people but with payouts too small to meet the most basic needs, particularly of the elderly.[31] Automation will help China avoid a sharp fall in productivity as its population ages, but it will be years before we know what that means for China's social safety net and the gov-ernment's ability to finance it.

All these pressures fuel the thousands of protests in China each year mentioned in the last chapter. The country's economic slowdown will make it much harder than in the past to address all these problems since the government's first priority will be to prevent the bankruptcy of deep-in-debt state-owned companies and local governments struggling to provide basic services for populations of people surging into cities. These are the kinds of issues that drive protest. As in other countries, those lifted from poverty have much higher expectations of government.

It's also possible that, if times get tough, China's middle class, and its consumption-driven lifestyle, will become a target—of poorer people who envy their prosperity and of a government looking to protect itself against populist anger. This fear within the middle class explains why so many send their children abroad for education and their money overseas for financial security. It may also explain why President Xi Jinping has explicitly revived the cult of personality around Mao Tse-tung, founder of the People's Republic and a man who wouldn't recognize the increasingly consumerist country that China has become. This is the fault line that might separate "us" and "them" within China if the country's economy suffers a major meltdown.

China has important advantages, particularly over other developing countries. First, its system of higher education is improving quickly and in ways that may help make the transition to a world of sharply expanded automation and artificial intelligence. According to annual rankings published by *U.S. News & World Report* in 2017, China is now home to four of the world's top ten engineering schools. (The United States also has four.) Each year, China now graduates four times as many students as the United States (1.3 million vs. 300,000) in the subjects of math, science, engineering, and technology.[32]

In addition, while India is uniquely diverse, the dominance of the majority Han Chinese population, which represents more than 90 percent of China's total population, creates social homogeneity in the country's most prosperous and influential cities and provinces. The lack of any viable leadership alternative to the Chinese Communist Party reinforces stability. It's also fortunate that China's senior leaders understand many of the country's challenges very well—and that the party's long-term survival depends on meeting them. No government has been more effective since 1980 in advancing reforms that expand prosperity. A serious effort is being made to tackle corruption, pollution, lack of access to education and decent medical care, wealth inequality, product (particularly food) safety, and the need for a stronger safety net.

But . . .

Though the Chinese leadership has said plenty about the positive impact that the large-scale introduction into the workplace of automation and artificial intelligence will have on China's economy, it has said and done little to address the enormous economic, social, and (perhaps) political turmoil it's bound to create. Remember that the World Bank has estimated that automation and innovations in machine learning threaten 77 percent of all existing jobs in China. That's a major disruption in the lives of hundreds of millions of people, particularly in the country's most crowded cities. As Chris Bryant and Elaine He wrote in January 2017, "It took 50 years for the world to install the first million industrial robots. The next million will take only eight, according to Macquarie [Group]. Importantly, much of the recent growth happened outside the U.S., in particular in China, which has an aging population and where wages have risen." China, they note, is installing a much bigger absolute number of industrial robots than any other country on earth.[33]

It's all the more remarkable, then, that China's political leaders say they're determined to embrace the tech revolution with both arms and as quickly as possible, with little public discussion of, or preparation for, massive job losses that can't be avoided. Instead, the government has focused almost exclusively on building China's competitive edge in robot manufacturing. In China's carefully controlled political system, there are no civil society organizations warning of this oncoming wave.

Xi Jinping's government will push hard to improve education for high-tech jobs, since China faces major shortages of high-skilled tech workers in semiconductors, robotics, and artificial intelligence. But there are also shortages of qualified teachers and open university slots, leaving huge numbers of workers with a fast-narrowing set of work options.

Failure to protect rising middle classes from crime, corruption, and contaminated food, air, and water, along with failure to care for the unemployed, sick, and elderly, creates a profoundly dangerous situation for China. But it is the extreme disruption of the workforce and massive loss of jobs that could push tens or hundreds of millions back toward poverty that might prove an entirely new kind of threat to the country's stability and its future.

China has some obvious advantages. It's the one government that, at least for now, can afford to spend huge amounts of money to create unnecessary jobs to avoid political unrest. China's historic successes suggest this might be the one country that can find a way to adjust, and the aging of its population could be a plus as the country needs fewer jobs in coming years than rival India. We all better hope so, because, month by month, the entire global economy is becoming more dependent on China's continued stability and growth.

Only now are the political implications of automation, the accelerating pace of machine learning, and the introduction into the workplace of artificial intelligence in developing countries beginning to become clear. Some of these governments will have the foresight, money, and talent they need to prepare young people to adapt to rapid technological change. Others won't have the money or the political will to act. Still others won't recognize the scale of the challenge. These are the factors that will determine which of these countries can survive and thrive.

The gap between winners and losers will also grow within individual countries, both developed and developing, as work that demands complex technical skills makes access to better schools and training more important than ever before. But we'll also see a reversal of globalization's great convergence as better schools and universities, more technically skilled citizens, stronger social safety nets, and stronger governing institutions will help wealthier countries cope much more effectively with these challenges. That's a problem for all twelve of these countries—and, therefore, for everybody else.

People and governments have demonstrated resilience throughout history, but the accelerating pace of technological change and its direct impact on so many lives and families around the world is driving the current international system headlong toward a reckoning.

Whether with creativity or by force, the state will build walls.

CHAPTER 4

WALLS

The future is already here.
It's just not evenly distributed yet.

—ATTRIBUTED TO WILLIAM GIBSON

Will walls kill democracy? Not for everyone. "Do walls work? Just ask Israel about walls," said Donald Trump in February 2017 in a reference to that country's four-hundred-mile security barrier on its border with the West Bank. Israel has also built walls and fences along part of its border with Egypt. Its Iron Dome, Arrow, and David's Sling missile defense systems add a ceiling to these walls by protecting citizens from incoming aerial attacks. It has invested in a floor in the form of a system designed to detect and destroy underground tunnels. Its security services have exceptional ability to track threatening communications and dangerous people through cyberspace, even in the occupied territories, where the risk of terrorist attack might otherwise be among the highest in the world.

Today, Israel appears more secure than at any time since its founding in 1948. It's the only truly stable democracy in the Middle East, one blessed with a free (often rambunctious) press, a world-class education system, rule of law, and independent governing institutions. Inside the walls, about 18 percent of Israeli citizens are Muslims, and they have the right to vote under Israeli law. Five of 120 members of the Knesset, Israel's parliament, are Sunni Muslims. Today, Israel's left struggles to rally its political base with calls for a peace settlement based on a "two-state solution," because arguments that Israel's long-term security depends on it have become more difficult to make.

In other words, Israel's walls work, if you're lucky enough to live inside them. The walls that separate Israel from Gaza and the West Bank make all the difference for quality of life. Outside them, per capita income is about $4,300. Inside, it's above $35,000. Unemployment is just under 18 percent in the West Bank and just over 42 percent in Gaza.[1] Inside the walls, it's just over 4 percent.[2] Youth unemployment outside the walls is 41 percent, but it's just 8.6 percent inside.[3] The infant mortality rate is 14.6 per 1,000 live births in the West Bank, 17.1 in Gaza, and 3.5 inside the walls. Less than 58 percent have Internet access outside the walls vs. nearly 80 percent inside.

Walls don't kill democracy. They protect democracy for "us" by denying it to "them." That's the argument that some will be making more openly in coming years in countries around the world. Walls are satisfying, and they make for good politics.

They're not hard to explain, and they offer a visible (if sometimes illusory) sign of security.

In many ways, we're talking about attempts to reverse the flow of globalization. To create the appearance of protecting jobs and industries, we'll see a continuing increase in garden-variety protectionism. We'll see more censorship—more restrictions, both old school and more innovative, on the transmission of information and politically resonant ideas. There will also be new barriers to the movement of people. The newest kinds of walls are those that will separate people within societies.

Some of these walls will be designed to protect "national interests," an idea that will be defined ever more broadly. Others will be built to protect the interests of a ruling party or even an individual leader and his family, friends, and clients. Some will be thrown up as quickly and haphazardly as the Berlin Wall, a barrier made of cheap cement and pebbles that divided East and West for twenty-eight years. Others will be digital-age barricades that are much more difficult to climb over or tunnel under.

PROTECTIONISM—IN ALL ITS FORMS

As governments try to safeguard the lives and livelihoods of citizens—and to protect themselves against public anger when their safeguards don't work—we can expect both old and new forms of economic protectionism. This is true even in wealthier countries, where citizens worry more about protecting existing prosperity than escaping poverty. The Depression-era policies of U.S. Presidents Herbert Hoover and Franklin Roosevelt reveal what becomes possible when economic desperation spills over into the politics of even a powerful and once self-confident country.

U.S. tariffs were already at historically high levels before Hoover responded to the 1929 stock market crash by signing the infamous Smoot-Hawley bill into law in June 1930. In the process, and over the public objections of hundreds of economists, the former commerce secretary approved a law that increased nearly nine hundred import duties.[4] Economists and politicians still debate the true importance of this step. Some say it deepened the Depression. Others say the impact of this single law has always been exaggerated. But Smoot-Hawley's biggest impact was in poisoning trade relations with other countries, provoking large-scale retaliation from Europe and Canada, and producing economic knots that took decades to untangle. According to Dartmouth economics professor Douglas Irwin, "When Congress was considering Smoot-Hawley in the 1930s, they didn't consider what other countries might do in reaction. They thought other countries would remain passive. But other countries don't remain passive."[5] Protectionism is contagious.

The 1930s offer other lessons as well. Roosevelt's career underlines dangers created by even the most well-meaning attempts to provide immediate help for desperate people. At the height of World War I, President Woodrow Wilson used the Trading with the Enemy Act of 1917 to expand the president's wartime economic powers. A generation later, Franklin Roosevelt expanded these capabilities to include peacetime "national economic emergencies." Congress quickly followed suit with the Emergency Banking Act, which gave government extraordinary powers to save the U.S. banking sector. Roosevelt used the National Recovery Administration, and its "Blue Eagle" program in particular, to name and shame private-sector companies that failed to follow government directives on everything from setting prices in line with government decree to hiring more people to reduce unemployment.[6] The government's official message wasn't subtle: "When every American housewife understands that the Blue Eagle [packaging logo] on everything that she permits into her home is a symbol of its restoration to security, may God have mercy on the man or group of men who attempt to trifle with this bird."[7]

The Blue Eagle program also required businesses to pay living wages, set limits on work hours, and end child labor—policies that were long overdue. But Roosevelt set a dangerous precedent for future presidents to declare states of economic emergency, giving them potent new powers that expand human suffering instead of easing it. Presidents can use these powers to force private companies into line with the policy of the moment, even when the plan is intended mainly to win votes rather than to restore long-term economic stability.

Franklin Roosevelt lifted American spirits with optimistic leadership and a sunny disposition through a dark period in U.S. history. In many ways, his New Deal alleviated the human misery of the Great Depression, and as democracies fell across Europe, we shouldn't underestimate the role that Roosevelt and his policies played in avoiding catastrophic political and social unrest in the United States. But it was World War II, not the New Deal, that brought economic stagnation to an end. U.S. unemployment was still at 19 percent during the recession of 1937–1938.[8]

More important, his overreach set dangerous peacetime precedents that future U.S. leaders might well use to score political wins in tough times.[9] This is a lesson from the United States, traditional champion of free enterprise, free trade, and political checks and balances—and a country where the story of Smoot-Hawley remains a cautionary tale. In other countries, both developed and developing, citizens are much less hostile to the idea of a heavy government hand in commerce and the construction of walls that restrict the flow of a modern economy's lifeblood.

Other walls are not as obvious. Where it's politically unpalatable or impossible to impose tariffs designed to boost the sale of domestic goods by making foreign products more expensive, lawmakers create nontariff barriers. They impose import quotas or strict product safety standards. They provide subsidies for domestic industries. To protect their affluence and advantages, wealthier countries treat science and technology as "strategic" economic sectors, restricting the export of new intellectual property. That leaves less innovative countries with fewer paths to boost growth. It's not just that poorer countries will get smaller pieces of the global economic pie. As protectionism lowers longer-term growth in rich countries, there is a risk the pie itself will get smaller, creating a vicious cycle as slowdowns increase demand for tough-talking populists in both rich and poor countries, leaders who will rise to power with promises of higher and thicker walls.

Many U.S. politicians have boosted their popularity with promises to oppose this or that trade deal, but no president since the 1930s has done more than Donald Trump to undermine the U.S. position on trade. His decision to withdraw the United States from leadership of the Trans-Pacific Partnership and promises to renegotiate the North American Free Trade Agreement and other existing deals have added momentum for anti-trade politics in both parties. Trade barriers in developed markets hurt living standards in middle-income countries like Mexico, Brazil, and South Africa that are heavily dependent on exports for revenue, at least as they try to shift strategies. The poorest countries will have a harder time borrowing in international markets. They'll face falling incomes, falling living standards, rising public anger, and political upheaval.

There are, of course, many examples of protectionism in developing countries themselves. As in wealthier countries, trade protectionism includes many nontariff restrictions. The fastest-growing economies of Southeast Asia, for example, have cut tariffs in half since 2000, but they're now more likely to use export bans, price controls, quality and health standards, and other strategies to protect local businesses and jobs. According to the UN Conference on Trade and Development, the number of nontariff barriers in place among the ten members of ASEAN jumped from 1,634 in 2000 to nearly 6,000 in 2015.[10] In short, both rich and would-be rich countries have signed trade agreements while still finding creative ways to protect local interests.

INFORMATION

In the twenty-first century, questions of trade and protectionism aren't limited to goods and services. Data has become an increasingly valuable and strategically important asset. The EU's General Data Protection Regulation, in effect from May 2018, requires that all companies that process personal data in the European Union follow strict rules on data privacy. Developing countries have gone further with restrictions on government procurement of both software and hardware from foreign companies. Data localization laws in these countries mandate that personal data generated in the country must be stored in the country. In this case, as elsewhere, risk-averse China is leading the way and countries like India, Brazil, Indonesia, Nigeria, and Russia are following, each for its own reasons. In some cases, these laws are intended to bolster national security, prevent espionage, and protect consumers from online criminals. But these rules and laws also restrict the free flow of information across borders and undermine the efficiency of global supply chains just like more traditional forms of protectionism.[11]

Governments will also build more walls to try to control the flow of more traditional forms of information across and within borders. In Egypt, China, and Turkey, the use of walls is literal, because these three countries imprison more journalists than any other. According to the Committee to Protect Journalists, Egypt jailed 25 journalists in 2016. China imprisoned 38, and Turkey incarcerated 81.[12] Around the world, there were 259 journalists in jail at the end of 2016, the highest number since 1990.[13] As the supply of bad news rises in line with the inability of governments to cope with looming economic, technological, and cultural changes, we can expect a lot more reporters to end up behind bars. To avoid this fate, many reporters will self-censor.

Instead of imprisoning individual journalists, it's often much more efficient to simply shut down the growing number of media outlets that report the news in ways that state officials don't like. To choose one of dozens of possible examples, in May 2017 the Egyptian government abruptly announced it had shut down twenty-one news websites that had been critical of the government. These websites were accused, predictably, of "spreading lies" and "supporting terrorism."[14] Among these websites was Al-Jazeera, a state-dominated news network based in Qatar that had frightened and angered governments across North Africa and the Middle East in 2011, first with coverage of the story of Tunisian vegetable vendor Mohammed Bouazizi and then of the advance across the region of the Arab Spring. Less than two weeks after Egypt banned these twenty-one sites, Saudi Arabia, the United Arab Emirates, Egypt, and Bahrain took the unprecedented step of severing all ties with Qatar, which they accused of supporting terrorist groups. Quarantine the reporter, quarantine the media outlet he works for, and, if possible, quarantine the government that backs them.

But journalists and websites are far from the only sources of information that the state might consider dangerous. Nongovernmental organizations that champion political, economic, and social reform have been shuttered in Russia, China, and even India. Among right-wing activists in the United States, George Soros, founder of the Open Society Foundations, a champion of freedom of expression, rule of law, and liberal democracy, has become a hated figure. The government of his native Hungary, led by the distinctly illiberal Viktor Orbán, has tried more than once to close Central European University, a school Soros founded. These sorts of walls will only become more common in a world where paranoid state officials fail to meet the most basic needs of citizens. As with more traditional forms of protectionism, these are (often hastily) improvised efforts to restore political stability at the expense of investment in long-term growth—economic, political, and intellectual.

Why attack individual sources of information when you can wall off the entire Internet? Of course, the fastest-shifting arena in the battle between the state and the flow of information is now in cyberspace, and the crudest tool that government can use to manage content is simply to shut down the Internet. During the Arab Spring, Hosni Mubarak's government became the first to disconnect the Internet across an entire country, a move made easier by the fact that Egypt, though it's home to more than 90 million people, has just a handful of Internet service providers.

To avoid major unrest and limit protests during politically sensitive events, India has shut down the Internet so often that it has itself become the focal point of a protest movement.[15] In response to riots in English-speaking regions of the West African nation of Cameroon, the government blacked out the Internet for three months—but only in regions that are home to most of the country's Anglophone minority. In response, Afrinic, the nonprofit that manages IP addresses for Africa, threatened to impose sanctions on governments that take these kinds of actions.[16] But at a time when both developed and developing states, democracies and dictatorships, face threats from terrorists and cybercriminals, sanctions against governments intensify debates over "Internet sovereignty," the right of lawmakers to regulate and police the Internet as they see fit. Are China and its imitators using censorship to protect their own political and economic power? Or are they simply taking steps that even the most open of democracies will have to follow in order to protect their citizens from terrorists, anarchists, and thieves? That's not an easy question. In the age of walls, the answer is both.

In Turkey, President Erdogan's government has become much more sophisticated in recent years in how it manages the Internet. Erdogan, like other thin-skinned leaders, has sometimes blocked Facebook, Twitter, and other social media tools that amplify the words of his critics, but some who use these sites have evaded these barriers by simply turning to virtual private networks (VPNs) and Tor, a tool that allows users to remain anonymous. In December 2016, however, the Turkish government began a crackdown on VPNs and Tor, according to Turkey Blocks, an Internet censorship watchdog.[17] According to a report issued by the group, "Partial or total blocking of VPN, Tor and similar services will shift Turkey's Internet censorship regime from moderate to severe in character, allowing the state fine-grained control of the flow of information in a 'walled garden' model of Internet access" to a degree comparable to state Internet management in China.[18]

Iran, another government intent on walling off information, announced plans several years ago to create a "Halal Internet," another form of information quarantine. In August 2016, Iran announced the opening of the "National Information Network," a move accompanied by the shutdown of a number of press agencies and news websites—and the arrest of more than a hundred Internet users, according to Reporters Without Borders (RSF), a freedom of information advocacy group. Iran's Committee for Determining Content that Supports Internet Crime launched this crackdown against individuals and organizations who had posted documents on corruption in city government in Tehran. According to RSF, "This National Information Network can be likened to a big Intranet, in which content is controlled and all users are identified, an Intranet that can be completely disconnected from the World Wide Web when the authorities so decide. It is a personal Internet or 'Halal Internet' based on 'intelligent filtering.'"[19]

Given that Vladimir Putin once referred to the Internet as a "CIA project," it's not surprising that his government has become fascinated with both its offensive capabilities and the internal vulnerabilities it might create for his control of information across Russia.[20] Before 2012, his government's drive to dominate the formation of Russian public opinion was limited mainly to control of content on television. That process continues, but a series of large-scale antigovernment protests in Moscow, organized through social media, got the Kremlin's attention. Beginning in 2012, the Russian government began granting itself the power to block online content as it saw fit.[21]

Since nationwide protests in 2017, described in the last chapter, the Russian government has broadened and quickened plans to police the Internet. Its strategy covers three areas: content controls, registration requirements, and control over infrastructure. It maintains a registry of banned web pages, forces media outlets to formally register with authorities, and has created broad data localization requirements that force companies to store data within Russia's borders. In November 2017, the government ordered foreign media to register as "foreign agents."[22] It is also creating a backup internal Internet that can be switched on and off by the government. Russian officials have threatened to fine or ban Western social media platforms and Internet sites that don't follow Russian law, and, as in China, the government works to promote domestic competitors to Western firms, companies that will be much easier for the Kremlin to control.

Russia, like all other countries not named China, faces an uphill battle to establish the degree of content dominance that an autocrat might want. Russia, like most developing countries, needs help in developing the IT infrastructure needed to remain economically competitive in a digital world. And, as in other countries, many Russian lawmakers don't understand the technologies they're trying to regulate. For now, Russia needs the expertise and IT services it can only get from foreign firms.

Yet Russia's government is finding new ways to manage politically sensitive content. Many Russians never read about the massive anticorruption protests in March 2017, at least not while the demonstrations were happening. Yandex News, the country largest news aggregator, uses an algorithm that prioritizes stories by the reliability of the media outlets that publish them. A Russian law enacted in January 2017 makes aggregators with more than a million daily users liable for all content that appears on their sites. Aggregators can bypass this requirement by promoting only source material that comes from media officially registered with Russia's media watchdog, Roskomnadzor.[23] Thus, if news doesn't make the Russian government's cut, it's much harder for Russian Internet users to find it anywhere online. Russia, like China, isn't just becoming less democratic. It's getting better at building walls.

China's leaders have proven (by far) the most innovative in the world in developing new ways of centralizing control of information—to the extent possible at a time when vast flows of ideas, information, and data cross borders, internal and external, at digital-age speed. As in all the countries discussed in this book, the Chinese leadership has multiple motives. It wants to provide security and prosperity for the Chinese people and to adapt to changing times by finding new ways to provide services to the public. It wants to protect China's national security and advance China's economic and political interests. But it also wants to ensure that the Chinese Communist Party maintains its monopoly hold on power by containing any potential internal challenger—particularly one that might become well organized.

In an era of unprecedented complexity in communications technology, China's leaders—like political officials everywhere—know they can't police every individual who criticizes, insults, or challenges the government. The ability of individual citizens everywhere to use new tools to broadcast their views, sometimes anonymously, guarantees some limited freedom of speech, even in China. But freedom of assembly is another matter. The Chinese government can't silence every angry voice, but it has many available methods and means to make sure those voices don't become a chorus.

In its drive for "cyber sovereignty," China's leaders use many tools. First, there are simpler ones, some of them old-fashioned. Regulations allow for tight government control of online news collection and distribution. Senior editors at approved media outlets receive state training and testing before they're allowed to work, and they face plenty of state scrutiny on the job. These rules apply not only to traditional media but also to social media platforms like WeChat that provide newslike services. Regulators periodically warn online information services like Sina, NetEase, Phoenix, and Tencent not to publish illegal news content. Google and Facebook are blocked.

There is a national security review for IT products and services used in critical information infrastructure, which is, not surprisingly, broadly defined. It is the patriotic responsibility of media and all who work in it to promote "positive propaganda." All must "strengthen and improve supervision over public opinion." From the official Xinhua news agency came this directive in May 2017: "Strike hard against online rumors, harmful information, fake news, news extortion, fake media and fake reporters."[24] In a future time of crisis, the state will define "harmful information" and what is "fake" in ways that promote the interests of the party first.

Then there are the Internet controls that have become familiar over the years. There is the "Great Firewall," which blocks access to tens of thousands of websites the Chinese government doesn't want citizens to see. The "Golden Shield" is an online surveillance system that uses keywords and other tools to shut down attempts to access content that the state considers politically sensitive. There is an ever expanding list of words and phrases that trigger denial messages online. More recently, China has moved on offense by introducing the "Great Cannon," which can alter content accessed online and attack websites that the state considers dangerous to China's security via a "dedicated denial of service" attack that can overwhelm servers to knock them offline.[25] There are also state cybercensors who track users that send messages using words or combinations of words on politically taboo subjects.[26] Later in this chapter, I'll detail the most ambitious (by far) of all the Chinese Communist Party's efforts to contain threats created by communication inside the country.

KEEPING THEM OUT

The past decade has proven again that the cross-border flow of ideas, information, money, goods, and services can have big political implications as it undermines the illusion of control that both leaders and citizens want to protect. But the flow of people is destabilizing in a much more immediate way. Even in the land of the Statue of Liberty, where Ellis Island romanticism has become part of the U.S. national identity, immigration remains a subject of bitter debate. In Europe, the principle of free movement of people through the Schengen area has become a central political concern, and the refusal of some EU members to accept union rules on quotas for Middle Eastern refugees offer early examples of a trend that will intensify.

Whether the question of the moment is jobs, terrorism, or the protection of national identity, governments around the world will become much more selective about who is allowed to enter. Large diaspora populations within countries will use their political clout to try to ensure that doors remain open to their compatriots. But immigration overall will become tighter. As job creation becomes a more sensitive subject in years to come, we can expect controversies over immigration even in developing countries, just as the flow of people from crisis-plagued Venezuela has already raised this issue even in Latin America.

In one important respect, future immigration debates will be different from those we've heard before. In the past, there was an obvious counterargument to immigration restrictions.

Proimmigration Americans, for example, aware that practical concerns and economic incentives are more persuasive for some people than moral arguments, have asserted that immigrants are needed to take the low-skilled work that few Americans want. Long before Trump glided down the Trump Tower escalator to warn Americans that Mexico was exporting "rapists" into the United States, Ronald Reagan promised to tighten controls at the southern U.S. border, and the number of illegal immigrants temporarily declined as a result. But it wasn't long before prices, particularly for food, began to rise as the drop-off in low-wage labor made agricultural products more expensive to produce. Pocketbook pain then eased political pressure on immigration, and border controls were relaxed.

Today, the argument is that low-wage construction workers, many of them immigrants from Latin America, boost American industry. But we're already living in a world where a 3-D printer can construct the foundation of a building in a matter of hours.[27] Whatever the industry, demand for lower-skilled, lower-wage labor will decline sharply in coming years in countries with access to this kind of technology. The moral and cultural arguments in favor of a more open approach to immigration are as strong as ever, but the economic argument is disintegrating, even in countries with fast-aging populations like Germany and Italy that need an influx of foreign migrant labor to power their economies forward. That's bad news for the countries that immigrants come from, where governments will face even greater pressure to create more jobs at home.

There are already a growing number of literal border walls

around the world. In fact, there are now more physical barriers at European borders than at any time during the Cold War. According to a 2016 report in *The Economist*, more than forty countries around the world have built fences against more than sixty of their neighbors since the fall of the Berlin Wall.[28] We see them in Asia, South America, and sub-Saharan Africa, as well as in Europe, the Middle East, and the United States. These obstacles leave poorer countries, like Jordan, and middle-income countries, like Greece and Turkey, to house huge numbers of migrants. The supply of refugees will grow as conflict, state failure, extreme climate conditions in poor countries, and the search for a better life push more and more people onto the road. The bottleneck countries can't absorb them all. As the problem builds, pressure will rise further inside wealthier countries for new walls that are higher and stronger.

In response, investment will flow toward new technologies. We can expect infrared sensors and cameras to update border controls.[29] Virtual walls will rise as well. We'll see wider use of biometric tools that allow governments to admit more of "us" and fewer of "them," however they are defined in each country. Governments will face public pressure to make citizenship harder to acquire. We'll hear more and louder calls to end "birthright citizenship," the legal right to citizenship in the country in which you are born, within countries that now honor it.

To welcome immigrants with skills and resources ahead of the wretched refuse knocking at the "golden door," citizenship will more often be for sale, and well-educated workers, particularly those with in-demand job skills, are more likely to have the money they need to buy visas.[30] In the United States, the EB-5 visa program already allows wealthy foreigners to accelerate their green card applications by investing hundreds of thousands of dollars in real estate projects.

In Europe, nearly half of EU members offer some form of investment residency or citizenship program. Today, these programs involve relatively small numbers of people, but as demand for restricted access rises within wealthier countries, these projects will expand.[31] Forced to become more creative, states will make wider use of "guest worker" programs that place new restrictions on the work that foreigners are allowed to do, their ability to change jobs, and their wages. As in apartheid South Africa, which required black and mixed-race citizens to live in townships that segregated them from the rest of the population, future "guest worker" programs will place similar restrictions on where foreign workers can live.

SORTING "US" FROM "THEM" WITHIN

We'll also see new methods of sorting citizens within states. Like so many of the trends described in this chapter, "identity politics" is an old story. Winning support by pitting one group of people against another is older than language. In Malaysia, discrimination that favors the ethnic Malay majority, two-thirds of the population, over ethnic Chinese, Indian, and other citizens is established in law. A day of deadly riots targeted at minorities in 1969 led to adoption of the New Economic Policy, which enshrined quotas for university admission and public-sector jobs. It's "affirmative action" for the majority, with all the positive and negative elements that come with that kind of plan. What was supposed to be temporary has become permanent, as officials in the United Malays National Organization, dominant players in the country's governing coalition, have discovered that discrimination in favor of the ethnic majority continues to win them elections. There are many other examples of this kind of politics around the world, and we'll see many more governments offering subtle and not-so-subtle changes to laws to concentrate power in the hands of those who will protect the government against "them."

There will also be new government efforts to establish greater control over the movement of people. In some countries, governments will try to establish new controls, or tighten existing ones, on the movement of people within borders. For years, Chinese citizens have lived with the *hukou* system, a registration list and internal passport that determines the opportunities and social provisions that a person can receive based on where he or she lives. Before 2014, a migrant from the countryside might pay taxes in the city to which he had moved for work, but could only receive public services and benefits in the province listed as his home. The same restrictions applied to his children, even if they were born in the city. The *hukou* was relaxed beginning in the 1980s to boost economic growth by allowing more movement of cheap labor toward urban factories, filling cities with huge numbers of second-class citizens. As a result, overcrowded cities have become increasingly difficult to govern, and the system has again been tightened to avoid urban chaos and the political problems it might create.

Today, Russia is the only other country that still uses a form of internal passport—something mainly associated with defunct systems like the Ottoman Empire, Soviet Union, or apartheid South Africa. But in a world of us vs. them, technological changes that give political officials access to unprecedented streams of data on citizens and their behavior will offer governments a tool that some will use to try to control the movement of people, particularly in volatile areas of the country. And, as we'll see later in this chapter, there are other ways in which governments could, theoretically, use data to increase the dependence of citizens on the state, allowing for greater political control in times of political crisis.

In the United States, divisions are growing more organically. Voting data from the 2016 U.S. presidential and congressional elections show increasingly sharp differences of political opinion depending on age, ethnicity, income, level of education, and whether the voter lives in a city or a rural area. These identities are interrelated, of course, and technological change will exacerbate these divisions in coming years by benefiting younger, better-educated people who live closer to centers of the modern job market and enjoy rising incomes as a result.

Over the years, there has also been a natural self-sorting process that separates one group from another.[32] Race is an obvious place to start. A 2013 study published in the journal *Education and Urban Society* found that "students are more racially segregated in [U.S.] schools today than they were in the late 1960s and prior to the enforcement of court-ordered desegregation in school districts across the country."[33] A 2013 study from Reuters/Ipsos found that "about 40 percent of white Americans and about 25 percent of non-white Americans are surrounded exclusively by friends of their own race."[34]

The updated 2016 edition of Paul Taylor's *The Next America: Boomers, Millennials, and the Looming Generational Showdown*, based on a collaboration with the Pew Research Center, provides a wealth of new data and offers a sobering look at the ongoing self-sorting of the United States. First, Taylor reports that racial, social, cultural, economic, religious, gender, generational, and technological changes are pushing Americans into "think-alike communities that reflect not only their politics but their demographics." Second, he notes that the United States will soon become a majority nonwhite nation, and that the percentage of older Americans is headed for record levels. Together, he writes, "these overhauls have led to stark demographic, ideological and cultural differences between the [two major political] parties' bases." Third, political divisions in America are widening. Taylor notes that "92 percent of Republicans are to the right of the median Democrat in their core social, economic and political views, while 94 percent of Democrats are to the left of the median Republican." In 1994, those numbers stood at just 64 percent and 70 percent, respectively. The same study in 2014 also found a doubling in the past two decades in the share of Americans with a highly negative view of the opposing party. Reinforcing the effect, "two-thirds of consistent conservatives and half of consistent liberals say most of their close friends share their political views."[35]

This self-sorting encourages both major political parties to send messages and adopt policies tailored to favored demographic groups to maximize their side's election day turnout while discouraging it on the other side, rather than to moderate core positions to draw support from centrist voters. In short, Republicans don't talk to Democratic voters, and Democrats don't talk to Republicans. The practice of gerrymandering, which allows state legislatures to draw the boundaries that separate congressional districts, has added to the us vs. them dynamic. As of February 2018, voters have given the Republican Party control of two-thirds of state legislatures and half of the nation's governorships. That allowed Republicans to win 55 percent of House seats in the 2016 congressional elections while winning just half of all votes cast.[36]

There are also efforts to use race to drive a political wedge between us and them. We saw this in President Trump's defense of white supremacists following violence during a protest over removal of Civil War statues in Charlottesville, Virginia. We saw it again with Trump's decision to pardon Arizona sheriff Joe Arpaio, who had been convicted of criminal contempt of court after refusing to comply with an order to end the harassment of people he believed, without evidence, to be illegal immigrants. We saw it again when Trump attacked the patriotism of professional football players who protested racism by refusing to stand for the national anthem before games. In each case,

Trump made a deliberate decision to arouse the anger of one group of Americans at another for personal political benefit. And he used race as his weapon.

WHO CHOOSES?

Then there's the question of who is allowed to vote. Remember that universal suffrage is a recent historical development even in Europe and America. The United States was founded as a democracy, but the Constitution allowed states to decide for themselves who deserved a vote. In the beginning, most states limited the franchise to white men who owned land and/or paid taxes. For everyone else, the nation functioned as an oligopoly. The industrial revolution began to change this as labor gained a voice in politics and workers gained a voice in the labor movement.

Only in 1856 did the last of the states drop the requirement to own property. In 1870, the Fifteenth Amendment to the Constitution extended voting rights to nonwhite men and freed slaves, though some states continued to violate this principle for nearly a century after. Women didn't win the vote until 1920. Only in 1924 were Native Americans allowed to vote without renouncing tribal affiliation. Much more progress was made in the mid-1960s. In 1964, the Twenty-Fourth Amendment finally prohibited states from using poll taxes in federal elections, a protection extended to all elections two years later. The landmark Voting Rights Act of 1965 protected minority citizens from discriminatory voting restrictions. In 1971, the increas-

ingly unpopular Vietnam War led to the Twenty-Sixth Amendment, which ensured that those young enough to fight were old
enough to vote.

But in 2013, the U.S. Supreme Court ruled that a crucial
section of the 1965 Voting Rights Act, which required state and
local governments to seek federal permission if they wanted to
change their voting laws, was unconstitutional.[37] Since then,
Republicans, aware that demographics offer long-term advantages for Democrats, have found new ways to protect their vote
share. According to an ongoing study by New York University
School of Law's Brennan Center for Justice, since the 2010 U.S.
congressional elections, lawmakers in many U.S. states have introduced new rules that make it harder to vote. According to
the report, "Twenty states have new restrictions in effect since
then—ten states have more restrictive voter ID laws in place
(and six states have strict photo ID requirements), seven have
laws making it harder for citizens to register, six cut back on
early voting days and hours, and three made it harder to restore
voting rights for people with past criminal convictions."[38] In the
2016 presidential election, the first held after the Supreme Court
ruling on the Voting Rights Act, fourteen states imposed new
voting restrictions for the first time in a presidential election.[39]

The battle over voting rights continues: In the first four
months of 2017, bills to expand access to registration and voting
were introduced in forty-five states, and bills to restrict these
rights were introduced in thirty-one states.[40] Those who favor
these policies claim they offer important protections against

voter fraud. Yet a study by the *Washington Post* found just four cases of voter fraud in 2016 following an election in which more than 135 million votes were cast. A 2014 study of elections from 2000 to 2014 found thirty-one cases of voter impersonation out of more than 1 billion votes cast.[41] In 2017, President Trump signed an executive order creating a commission on "election integrity" to bolster his baseless claim that "millions" of people had voted illegally for his opponent in the 2016 election.[42] There is also an attempt by some, including Trump, to nudge people away from voting. If you can't make it impossible for someone to vote, you can always make it more difficult. Increase the number of documents that must be obtained. Find ways to lengthen voting lines. Target messages to discourage certain voters.

NEW TOOLS, NEW WEAPONS

In 2009, the Indian government, then led by the Indian National Congress Party, enabled the creation of Aadhaar, a biometric identification system. In 2010, the program began recording iris scans and fingerprints as a way of establishing each person's unique identity. Each user is given a unique twelve-digit ID number, and well over one billion people are now listed in the Aadhaar database. When the program is completed, everyone will receive his or her own benefits, subsidy fraud will become much more difficult to pull off, the government can collect more taxes and waste much less money, and all can have confidence in their access to essential services. Payments already flow automatically into and out of citizens' bank accounts, even in India's most isolated rural areas.

In the beginning, the program was voluntary, and its creators promised it would remain so. But the government of current Prime Minister Narendra Modi has larger ambitions. He wants required Aadhaar membership to ensure that kids enroll in school and receive free lunches during the school day, for workers to prove their attendance on the job and pay their taxes, for the poor to receive welfare benefits, for consumers to buy a train ticket or a new phone, and for the elderly to receive pension payments. Not surprisingly, the system has had its share of early problems. Access to the system, needed to prove identity, depends on access to electricity and an Internet connection. Both, as I wrote in the last chapter, remain works in progress in developing India. There's also the risk that centralizing so much personal information in a single database will leave India, its citizens, and its political stability vulnerable to various forms of cyberattack.

But there's another question. There is no good reason to accuse the previous or current Indian government of amassing all this data to control the population by, for example, cutting subsidies, payments, and services to the Aadhaar-connected bank accounts of people who criticize or otherwise challenge the government. India is a dynamic democracy, and its courts continue to try to set limits on Aadhaar's requirements. But for government, the potential for unprecedented control and abuse exists. It's true that the government has long had access to personal information on a big part of the population, but only now does it have a single central database with direct access to information about—and bank account access to—the lives of more than one billion people. Armed with a powerful weapon that can serve as a wall of protection between the state and the nation's people—particularly in areas where government is especially unpopular—future leaders will be tempted to use it.[43]

Then there is China's new "reputation system." What can people learn about you by looking at your credit score? They can see whether you pay your bills on time, how many credit cards you hold, how much money you've borrowed, and whether you've ever defaulted on a loan or filed for bankruptcy. They can see whether you've borrowed to buy a home and the addresses where you've lived. They can see if you've borrowed to go to school and make a rough guess at how much money you have. A good credit score allows you to borrow money and pay it back at a lower interest rate. A bad score can force you to pay much higher interest or block you from borrowing altogether.

In China, the state is now experimenting with something new, a "social credit system." Imagine a credit report that reveals whether you've ever committed a felony. Or recently committed a misdemeanor. Or been arrested. Or been caught cheating on a test. Whether you have traffic violations and if you've paid your fines on time. Whether you've ever been drunk in public. Whether you've ever missed an alimony or child support payment. Whether you often visit your elderly parents. Whether you've been fired from a job and why you were fired.

Other questions your social credit report might answer:

Have you ever volunteered in your community or received honors from the government for service to your country? Have you ever signed a petition? What did the petition say? Have you visited undesirable websites? Have you been photographed at a protest? What were you protesting? Have you ever written something on the Internet that had to be censored or that led administrators to question your loyalty to the state? Do you have friends with any of these bad habits? If so, have you tried to change their minds? The state may have no plans to use all these questions in the first version of its social credit system, but when times are tough and unrest is on the rise, a strong state with access to lots of data could expand the system.

A good social credit score might help you win a promotion, a raise, a better apartment, better schools, access to state-approved dating websites, better stores that offer better goods and services, better doctors, the right to travel, a more generous pension, or important opportunities for your children. A bad score could put you in jail. This is not an entirely new idea. The *hukou* registration, mentioned earlier, and the collection of personal reports at school and work have long been part of Chinese life. They still are. But the social credit system will put digital-age tools of social control in the hands of those who might one day use them because they badly need them. This in a world where advanced computers now process vast amounts of written and spoken language, and software engineers have created computer programs that recognize individual faces in very large crowds.

China's social credit project remains at an early stage of development, though dozens of local governments have already begun to amass digital records of various forms of personal behavior. The plan is to go nationwide with an early version by 2020. We can't know yet how intrusive the information requests will be, or whether it will be possible to apply it to everyone or only to certain groups of people. Planners haven't yet decided how much information they can demand without provoking a public backlash. Will the Chinese people push back, forcing limitations on its use?

Nor should we underestimate the technical challenge in building this kind of system. When it comes to opinions expressed online, those who run the system will have to match individual messages with the owners of the devices that generated them. Under Chinese law, Internet providers must maintain the real names and personal information of all customers, but those looking to beat the system—the people the state should worry most about—rarely provide their real names, and some use virtual private networks to hide their IP addresses. Is it possible to collect enough data to realize the plan's full potential? Or maybe the system will produce far more data than can be effectively analyzed without making millions of mistakes.

A lot of good can come from this system. It can make government more aware of what people want and more accountable for providing it. People want social credit. They want to know that government can provide access to the good things in life. They want to be signed up for services. The system can also be used to punish people who cheat fellow citizens, restaurants that serve contaminated food, and companies that make defective and dangerous products or pollute the country's air and water. All these problems are commonplace in China. As in India, development and use of these kinds of tools is not, and will never be, a black-and-white issue.

But the potential for intrusion into 1.4 billion personal lives is unprecedented. Published information on the plan says it's intended as a safeguard against, among other things, "conduct that seriously undermines . . . the normal social order" and "assembling to disrupt social order [and] endangering national defense interests." The plan's ultimate purpose, according to Chinese officials, is to "allow the trustworthy to roam everywhere under heaven while making it hard for the discredited to take a single step." That sounds Orwellian enough, but it also says a lot about how the system might one day work, particularly in a world where even the most basic tasks become harder to accomplish without an Internet connection over which government can exert more control.[44]

The social credit system is a tool the state can use to decide whether it can trust you. If it trusts you, your horizons are limitless. If the state cannot trust you, you're not going anywhere. China is a one-party state. Its leaders can decide for themselves how this system will and will not be used without worry that a court will rule their new powers unconstitutional. They are accountable only to one another—for as long as they're able to contain dissent.

There's never before been a wall like this.

CHAPTER 5

NEW DEALS

Necessity is the mother of (re)invention.

—ADAPTED FROM PLATO

There is another way.

It's inevitable that some governments will build walls. Others—those with the will, the means, and the inclination— will experiment with new ways of ensuring that the needs of the public are met, even if government itself is only part of the solution.

You're a citizen who pays your taxes and abides by the law. What does your government owe you in return? Expectations of government vary enormously from one society to another. Some say the law's primary purpose is to define the rights of the individual and to protect citizens from government overreach. Others insist that it's the collective that matters most, and that government's responsibility is to promote national values and a healthy society. Some say the state must safeguard the rights of citizens against the predations of profit-hungry corporations, while others assert that business drives prosperity for all and that government's main responsibility is to stay out of the way.

Is the purpose of government to bring about change, to enable others to bring about change, or to protect society against the worst effects of change? Some will say there's a place for all three of these roles. There are big differences of opinion on all these questions across countries, within communities, and even inside families, but given the irreversible changes under way in our world, it has never been more important to look closely at all our assumptions about the social contract: the agreement between the state and the individual that binds societies together.

There's one value that virtually everyone shares: the belief that government has a duty to safeguard the personal security of each citizen—though "security" can be defined narrowly or broadly. You expect government to honor and protect the rights guaranteed to you by your nation's constitution. If you're accused of a crime, you expect to receive all the protections afforded you by law. If you're a victim of crime, you expect justice. You expect safeguards against crime and corruption—and that government will protect you from threats from beyond the nation's borders. These days, that's often less about the invasion of a foreign army than about trade policies and intrusions of various kinds in cyberspace. Some expect their leaders to pursue a foreign policy that advances the national interest—and, by extension, their personal security and opportunity for prosperity.

What else do citizens expect? The U.S. Declaration of Independence offers this partial definition of the social contract:

> We hold these truths to be self-evident, that all men are created equal, that they are endowed by their Creator with certain unalienable Rights, that among these are Life, Liberty and the pursuit of Happiness.—That to secure these rights, Governments are instituted among Men, deriving their just powers from the consent of the governed,—That whenever any Form of Government becomes destructive of these ends, it is the Right of the People to alter or to abolish it, and to institute new Government, laying its foundation on such principles and organizing its powers in such form, as to them shall seem most likely to effect their Safety and Happiness.

God has given you life, freedom, and a chance to be happy. Government's job is to ensure that no one takes these rights away from you, and if government fails in its responsibility—or if government itself denies you your rights—you have the God-given right to bring the government crashing down.

Thomas Jefferson used these ideas to justify, on behalf of American colonists, a declaration of formal separation from the British Empire. Yet the Fifth and Fourteenth Amendments to the U.S. Constitution protect the right to life, liberty, and "property," a formulation inspired directly by the seventeenth-century political philosopher John Locke. Locke and Jefferson agreed that God was the source of these rights, and that government had no right to take them away. Today, even those who don't believe in God, or who believe that God has no place in politics, can insist that some rights are "unalienable" and that government's role is to protect them. But the Universal Declaration of Human Rights, adopted at the formation of the United Nations, insists on the right to life, liberty, and "security of person." In other words, when it comes to the social contract, even the basics are up for debate.

It's important to remember that the idea of a social contract is not the invention of Enlightenment-era European philosophers. The Arthashastra of ancient India, credited to the philosopher and economist Kautilya, though authored in Sanskrit by many people over the two centuries before and after Christ, offered early ideas on this subject. These writings assert that taxes are paid in exchange for services rendered by the king, and that the king's duty, consistent with the Hindu scriptures, is to ensure the welfare and material well-being of his subjects. There are many other examples of this idea throughout history and across East and West that long predate Jean-Jacques Rousseau, Thomas Hobbes, Locke, and Jefferson.

What else do you expect from government? A job? An opportunity to provide for your children and to give them a better life than you've had? Does government owe you an education? A chance to use your mind after you've graduated? How about safe roads and bridges and ports and airports? Safe drinking water? Internet infrastructure that protects your property and privacy? At affordable prices? How about access to medical care? If your child will die without medical treatment, does government owe her access to a doctor? At a cost that's within your means? How about care in old age?

Does government owe you a say in government? Elections that are conducted freely and fairly? Access to unbiased information? Freedom of speech? Does it have some responsibility to place limits on that freedom for the good of society? Freedom of assembly? What if some citizens use their freedom of assembly to organize protests that block your drive to work? Does government have an obligation to protect citizens whose gender, ethnicity, religion, or sexual orientation have opened them to past discrimination, whether by government or by other citizens? A nation's constitution may answer many of these questions, but as times change, values evolve, and technology creates opportunities and problems that the document's original authors could never have imagined, how are rights to be updated?

Whatever your answers to these questions, it's clear that government's obligations under the social contract extend well beyond national security and a shot at a better life. A government's legitimacy rests on many things, and readers who are citizens of genuine democracies will surely answer these questions differently than citizens of China, Russia, or Saudi Arabia. But even autocrats must worry about public opinion—and about whether a significant number of citizens have come to believe that their government is unwilling or unable to meet their most basic needs.

Come back to the "pursuit of happiness." What makes people happy, or at least boosts their sense of well-being? Since 2012, a United Nations agency has been trying to find out. The

2017 World Happiness Report offers some interesting answers.[1] The study's authors found seven factors that make people most happy: "caring, freedom, generosity, honesty, health, income and good governance." Some of that sounds a little abstract, and only the last of these refers directly to political officials, but all seven tell us something about what people expect from government. They want leaders who care what happens to them, who treat them with dignity, and who don't interfere in their lives or punish them arbitrarily. They want leaders who will help them when no one else can, who are honest, who can create and sustain a system that provides economic opportunities, and who know what they're doing. Whether you're a libertarian or a Marxist, that definition of government's end of the social contract works pretty well.

Scandinavian countries continue to dominate the UN rankings. There are various theories about why that is, but these are countries in which citizens are burdened with relatively high taxes. Perhaps they're more confident than people in other parts of the world that their tax money will be well spent, and that they're investing in programs like free university education, free health care, and other social protections that provide a direct and immediate boost to personal security, quality of life, and the health of society as a whole. Whatever the case, the high taxes that come with their definition of the contract don't appear to be weighing them down.

Then there's what China's President Xi Jinping calls "the Chinese Dream." There's no simple definition of this idea. Xi describes it differently to different audiences, but it's mainly his personal vision of China's revival and peaceful rise toward greatness. It's a dream of strength, independence, modernity, creativity, self-reliance, and power. It's rooted in history and tradition. And it's a response to perceived national humiliations visited upon the country by outsiders from the mid-nineteenth century to the mid-twentieth. Xi's Chinese Dream differs from the American Dream in one important, if entirely predictable, way: Its central actor is not the individual or the family but a strong and disciplined ruling party at the vanguard of the Chinese people. The American version of the social contract generally requires that government recognize the unalienable rights of the citizen. The Chinese Dream centers on the ability of the state to lift the Chinese people up and lead them forward.

That UN World Happiness Report ranks the United States at 14 in the world, while China comes in at 79, but that doesn't necessarily tell us how Chinese people feel about their government. Per capita income and life expectancy in China are still much lower than in the United States, though China's state-directed economic reform process has lifted hundreds of millions of people out of poverty over the past thirty years. And China's ranking has held steady over time in the index. Much more to the point, there has been no recurrence of the 1989 Tiananmen Square mass demonstrations that might have split the ruling party in two and provoked nationwide upheaval. We're not allowed to ask Chinese people how they feel about Communist Party rule, and they're not allowed to tell us. But it matters whether the party delivers on its promises, because even an autocrat violates the social contract at his peril.

Is there a Russian Dream that might help us understand how today's Russian understands the social contract? Historically, Russian/Soviet law existed to protect the state from the dangers posed by individuals who challenged its authority, not the other way around. On paper, that's no longer the case. But the decisions of judges in today's Russia are not always determined by the law, and corruption remains a serious problem in a country dominated by a very few wealthy and powerful people. In addition, Russia has been mired for the past several years in an economic slowdown, and polling suggests that most of its people don't expect better economic times ahead.

So what gives the still popular Vladimir Putin and his government their legitimacy? Are the citizens of Russia and other countries willing to endure significant hardship without challenging their government's right to rule? Public expectation of government changes over time, of course, especially in response to bouts of hardship. In a poll conducted in March 2017 by Moscow's Levada Center, 31 percent of respondents agreed that "the state gives a lot, but we can demand more," a 6 percent rise over the previous year. Another 31 percent, also up 6 percent, agreed with the statement that "the state gives so little that we owe it nothing." Those who indicated a belief that the citizen has a responsibility to help the state, even if it requires personal sacrifice, also fell by 6 percent.* It's said that Putin has restored the pride and dignity that Russians lost with the collapse of the

---

*"Quarter of Russians put state interests above personal rights, poll shows," rt.com, April 3, 2017. www.rt.com/politics/383189-quarter-of-russians-put-state/.

Soviet empire and the frightening economic chaos that followed. Where do pride and dignity figure in the social contract? Despite recent hardships, Putin has maintained an approval rating above 80 percent over several years.

But in the United States, Scandinavia, China, and Russia, how long can today's agreement between the state and the individual last?

REWRITING THE SOCIAL CONTRACT

Faced with the challenges to come, there are things that (some) governments can do to rebuild relationships with their citizens. In short, they can rewrite the social contract to provide for the needs of society in new ways. Inequality will become a prime target of these changes. There will always be rich and poor, but history has shown again and again that when the gap between them becomes too wide, and when there are too few people in the middle, trouble follows. That's why the United States, like many other countries, has a "progressive" tax system, one in which wealthier people pay income tax at a higher rate than poor people, and why taxes paid at every income level go to provide services for those who can't afford them, to limited-term insurance payments for the unemployed, and to pensions and health care for the elderly.

The United States existed for almost a century before the first large-scale effort was made to provide for people in their most vulnerable stages of life. The private sector, not government, led the way. The first pensions in America were provided by the American Express Company to its employees in 1875. By 1919, there were three hundred private pension plans, covering about 15 percent of wage and salary employees in the United States, but until the 1930s few Americans had any expectation that someone outside the family would help the elderly pay to live out their lives.

At the height of economic depression in 1935, the Roosevelt administration created the Social Security system, which Americans pay into during working years and draw from after they retire. The age of retirement was set at sixty-five at a time when life expectancy was about sixty.[2] For years after, companies hoping to attract talented workers continued to offer "defined-benefit" pension plans that promised specific amounts of money for retirement, but a growing realization that companies would not be able to control the resulting costs led them to offer "defined-contribution" plans that allowed workers to invest more of their own money. In 1978, Congress allowed for the establishment of 401(k)s that enable employees to contribute pretax income to private pension plans. As life expectancy has increased, various forms of individual retirement accounts have developed with different sets of tax requirements.[3] In short, as public expectation of government increased, U.S. political leaders understood the need to adapt, to find new ways to share burdens among the state, citizens, and the private sector. Solutions will take different forms in different times and places, but around the world, the need for these types of changes is about to rise with new urgency.

Rewriting the social contract to help people survive and thrive in dangerous times also means rethinking assumptions about the purpose and content of education—and how it's provided. It means fundamental changes in the way that governments collect taxes. It means preparing people to compete and succeed in a fast-changing economy and providing for their most basic needs when they don't or can't. It means welcoming creative thinking on the broader challenge from those inside and outside government. And it requires that government work with private companies and institutions to meet the moment.

EDUCATION

Opportunity begins with education, which must now become a lifelong process. First, preparing people to succeed in a digital-age economy does not require abandonment of a traditional liberal arts education. In fact, given the ever growing importance of critical thinking, creativity, and the ability to communicate with a much more diverse range of people over the course of a working life, an education that includes history, philosophy, literature, art, and music as well as math, science, and digital skills will be more important than ever.

In addition, multiple studies in recent years have shown that access to early education is a critical component in battling income inequality and all sorts of other social problems.[4] It will play a vital role in fostering the adaptability of human beings to a faster-changing world. For many, early childhood education will be a new expense, and government has finite resources, but this is a crucial area of investment in a nation's ability to compete in a global knowledge economy. Where national governments fail, local governments can succeed. A state, province, city, or town that offers affordable early education can attract smart, talented parents who want to ensure their children have the best chance to succeed. New York City has invested in universal prekindergarten education that brings 70,000 children into the classroom at age four, giving them the opportunity to learn while relieving their working parents of the cost of private school or day care programs.[5]

But education must extend far beyond youth. The increasing speed of technological change ensures that workers must learn new skills quickly and often, and that workers will be asked to shift jobs, and even industries, much more often than ever before. By providing access, or incentivizing others to provide access, to training and retraining on an historically unprecedented scale, governments can help citizens make most of the opportunities that change creates. In Singapore, a government agency called Workforce Singapore works with businesses to retrain their employees by helping them develop the new skills needed to remain valuable.[6]

Whether for young children or mature adults, education can't simply be about sitting in a classroom, important as that experience is. Distance learning will be a critical component of education at every age. The role of government here is to ensure that citizens can afford all these levels of education, and that the technology is available to them. In Singapore, government has created "individual learning accounts" to provide every citizen over twenty-five with money to spend on training in new technologies.[7] There will be many more such experiments, large and small, in coming years around the world, and those who lead the way will reap the first benefits.

TAXES

Governments will also have to consider new ideas on taxes. As we've seen, the automated workplace of the future will have a lot fewer people in it, and the people who are there will have different skill sets. In an earlier chapter, I noted the unavoidable impact of the coming of automation. How can government use the large-scale advent of automation to bolster its end of the social contract bargain? Many on the European left have called for a tax on robots, but the idea gained a much wider audience when Microsoft cofounder Bill Gates endorsed the idea to pay for the retraining of workers who can be retrained and for the displacement costs of those who can't. Employ more people and pay higher salaries for those who teach our children and care for the elderly, two jobs for which human beings, not robots, will be needed for years to come. In managing this process, there's an important role for government, Gates has argued. "If you want to do [something about] inequity, a lot of the excess labor is going to need to go help the people who have lower incomes. And so it means that you can amp up social services for old people and handicapped people and you can take the education sector and put more labor in there. Yes, some of it will go to, 'Hey, we'll be richer and people will buy more things.' But the inequity-solving part, absolutely government's got a big role to play there."[8]

Former U.S. Treasury Secretary Larry Summers has some good counterarguments. What's special about robots? he has asked. If you're going to tax their use, why not tax all the machines that industry uses for work that a person could perform? And why discourage useful innovations? In a world of driverless cars, for example, deadly accidents will be much less common, and robotics can help doctors perform life-saving operations that would be impossible without them. So why respond to the businesses who create these valuable tools by raising their taxes? And won't taxes on technology push companies to move operations to places where governments don't impose these sorts of penalties? That won't create jobs at home. Finally, Summers asks, "Why tax in ways that reduce the size of the pie rather than ways that assure that the larger pie is well distributed? Imagine that 50 people can produce robots who will do the work of 100. A sufficiently high tax on robots would prevent them from being produced. Surely it would be better for society to instead enjoy the extra output and establish suitable taxes and transfers to protect displaced workers?"[9] There are strong points on both sides, and this is a debate that government should be having in every country where automation of the economy will have a major political impact. That is, everywhere.

As this debate highlights, government must decide whether

its tax policies should be designed to boost employment or standards of living for consumers. The two approaches are not at all mutually exclusive, but policy priorities must be coherent to accomplish either goal. To incentivize job creation, governments could tax corporations based on the revenue they earn rather than the number of workers they employ. Or, as Ruchir Sharma argues in his book *The Rise and Fall of Nations*, maybe government should base tax rates on the ways in which money is made rather than how much is made. To encourage innovations that raise standards of living for consumers, government could impose higher tax rates on income earned from rents than from those earned through innovations. Those who invent useful new things should be treated differently than those who earn money without adding to productivity. All these ideas and more should be part of the debate.

There is also the inconvenient problem of debt. Whether the question centers on indebted nations, like Greece, or indebted citizens, like students paying off the enormous loans they've taken out to earn a degree at a time of fast-rising tuition costs, debt has cast a long shadow over the future of national economies and global markets. Rewarding those who spend too much and save too little by writing down debt is a dangerous business. That has not changed. But, as Mohamed El-Erian has warned, "the alternatives are worse."[10] Default serves no one, and a carefully negotiated approach to debt can benefit both lenders and borrowers, ensuring that both have the means to fulfill their own social contracts.

THE GIG ECONOMY

Given the increasing speed of automation of the workplace and other trends, some governments will experiment with the creation of incentives for participation in the "gig economy," one in which individuals accept a life of freelance work because they don't want (or can't find) full-time work for a single employer. This is not a fad: In Europe, half of all jobs created between 2010 and 2016 were based on temporary contracts.[11] That's in part a reflection of an economic slowdown across the EU that left employers wary about full-time hires, but the automation trend suggests there will be fewer new jobs created in the future, even when times are strong. Whether we view the gig economy as a solution or a coping mechanism, it's here, and the people who participate in it have different needs than those with full-time work.

As people working in gig economy jobs—as Uber drivers, Airbnb hosts, or part-time workers in any field—struggle to build families, buy homes, educate their children, find affordable health insurance, care for aging parents, and save for their own futures, governments, citizens, and companies must find new ways to provide for the basic needs of the individual. In a digital-age economy, it's not a matter of cutting better trade deals. A reorganization of the social safety net will be required whether we like it or not.

In Denmark, Prime Minister Løkke Rasmussen has created a state "Disruption Council," which consists of the prime minister, a diverse group of government ministers, business leaders, and policy experts, to find new ways to ensure that as new technologies power the economy forward, the state can help workers adapt. "When some working tasks disappear, we need to find new ones," said Rasmussen in 2017. In this case, "we" means Denmark's government. "The community must give a helping hand to those left behind by the technological giant leaps. If not, our society will disintegrate," added his employment minister.[12]

Another idea gaining ground in Europe is the concept of "guaranteed basic income." The idea is simple: If you believe that the gig economy will be the future of work for huge numbers of people, government will have to find new ways to encourage people to accept this work by making it possible to build a life and a family on this foundation. Some unemployed people refuse to even look for part-time work because the salaries on offer aren't much more appealing than the benefits they have to give up to take these jobs. They remain on the dole. They pay little or no taxes. Their services are provided almost entirely by the state. They have little sense of self-worth.

What if the state provides these people with a small amount of income? Not enough to live well, but enough to survive, and tells them that the checks will keep coming even if they take a job. In that way, people can afford to take part-time or freelance work to contribute their talents to society, generate economic growth, pay taxes, and provide for themselves and others. Or maybe the income allows them to care for their sick children or aging parents. That work has value for society as well.

Finland's government has experimented with exactly this kind of guaranteed income plan. As part of a trial, it sent monthly tax-free payments of €560 (about $600) to 2,000 unemployed citizens chosen at random. The plan is also designed to cut bureaucracy, because guaranteed income doesn't require state employees to build and maintain a complex database to track the continuing eligibility of participants. Variations on this idea have the attention of policymakers in many countries. Though Swiss citizens voted in a referendum in 2016 to reject a plan that would have provided a minimum income to every citizen, local governments in Canada, the Netherlands, Scotland, Brazil, and Oakland, California, have experimented with this idea for the unemployed.[13] Also in 2016, French presidential candidate Benoît Hamon ran on promises to launch a similar plan in his country that would be financed by a tax on the use of robots in the workplace.[14] Some have advanced the idea of universal basic income, cash payments designed to provide everyone in society a survival wage as people navigate all the coming changes in the workplace.

Let's stop right here. If you're an American, maybe you're shocked by the idea that anyone would suggest that the state should pay people who don't work to earn the money. But if the guaranteed income idea seems totally antithetical to an American work-ethic-driven culture, consider that founding father Thomas Paine proposed in 1797:

To create a national fund, out of which there shall be paid to every person, when arrived at the age of twenty-one years, the sum of fifteen pounds sterling, as a compensation in part, for the loss of his or her natural inheritance, by the introduction of the system of landed property:

And also, the sum of ten pounds per annum, during life, to every person now living, of the age of fifty years, and to all others as they shall arrive at that age.[15]

Nor is this simply an eighteenth-century idea. President Richard Nixon first proposed a modest version of partial basic income in 1968, and his plan passed the House of Representatives before dying in the Senate, where Republicans opposed the plan's cost and Democrats complained it wouldn't help enough people.[16] Friedrich Hayek, an economist revered by many American libertarians for his belief in individual freedom and minimal government, wrote, "I have always said that I am in favor of a minimum income for every person in the country."[17] Elsewhere, he described the idea as "a certain minimum income for everyone . . . a sort of floor below which nobody need fall even when he is unable to provide for himself."[18]

In 1975, Congress created the Earned Income Tax Credit, an idea advanced by economist Milton Friedman, a hero to many American conservatives, to provide financial support in inverse proportion to a worker's income.[19] That kind of program would be a nonstarter in today's Washington, but even this idea falls far short of the challenge of coping with the advent of the gig economy. The subsidies this tax credit provides can help lift people out of poverty—no small thing—but the benefit phases out as incomes rise, reducing a worker's incentive to find a higher-wage job. Guaranteed basic income might help with this problem.

REINVENTION

There are other ideas that can help. In Singapore, many workers and their employers contribute a considerable percentage of their income to the so-called Central Provident Fund. This money creates accounts from which citizens can borrow to put down deposits on state-built apartments. Mortgages are then paid directly from their fund accounts, and apartments are heavily subsidized for first-time home buyers. In this way, the fund provides housing and savings for old age.[20]

There have been much more ambitious plans to reduce inequality and bring more people into the economy. In 2000, about one-third of Brazilians lived below the international poverty line. The Workers Party came to power in Brazil in 2003 on promises to lift large numbers of these people out of poverty and hunger while making productive citizens of those who had never participated in the economic life of their country. President Luiz Inácio Lula da Silva created a program called Fome Zero (Zero Hunger) to invest in providing poor people with affordable food, access to water, basic health information, access to small amounts of credit, and support for small-scale farming. It also included a program called Bolsa Familia (Family Grant), which consisted mainly of cash payments that poor people could receive only if they vaccinated their children against disease and sent them to school. By 2014, this relatively low-cost program had cut the number of Brazilians living in poverty by two-thirds and provided millions of young people with unprecedented opportunities to learn. Beyond these obvious benefits, many experts who have looked closely at its costs say the program overall is efficient, cost-effective, and generally free of corruption in a country that has spent the past several years mired in the worst corruption scandal in the country's history.[21]

India has built on this model. Return to the country's Aadhaar biometric identification system described in the last chapter. As part of a program called Jan Dhan, it has also been used to transfer cash directly into the bank accounts of people otherwise unable to afford banking fees or maintain minimum balances. Payments into the system are small, intended only to help people survive. Administering money transfers, tax returns, health insurance, and other benefits directly through this system cuts enormous amounts of waste from India's notoriously complicated state bureaucracy and virtually eliminates opportunities for official corruption, an enormous burden in India as in most other developing countries. It also reduces fraud because its use of biometric identification helps prevent one person from stealing another's benefits. The program is essentially intended to remove all middlemen in relations between the citizen and the state.

There are downsides, potential and actual, in all these ideas. Will a person who receives guaranteed income still look for work? Knowing that benefits won't be lost can make a difference, in theory, but until variations of the basic income idea are tested, adapted, and tested again, we won't know whether it can work on a large scale. Let's also remember that the Saudi economy is, in a sense, nationwide guaranteed basic income. The government doesn't tax citizens, and it provides large numbers of people with undemanding state-sector jobs to give them a stake in the stability of one of the world's least innovative and dynamic economies. In 2015, state salaries and various allowances and other perks accounted for nearly half the kingdom's state budget.[22] In addition, the Saudi government treats this system as if its willingness to provide for citizens in this way relieves those in power of any obligation to give citizens a greater say in how they're governed.

Singapore's housing scheme is notoriously complicated and leaves a large percentage of people's income tied up in their homes. Bolsa Familia can educate huge numbers of young people and bring them into the job market, but if there are no jobs for them, relations between citizens and the state will become much worse. And by creating a central database in India to connect people directly with government, Aadhaar planners have created one of the world's largest targets of opportunity for disruptive hacking. Huge numbers of citizens could find themselves cut off from basic services if their personal data and identities are stolen. Programs like these in developing countries can lift people into middle classes, but it can't necessarily keep them there. We'll never learn what works, what doesn't, and why until these ideas are tested in different societies with different needs.

There are also smaller steps that government can take to help citizens transition toward the demands of twenty-first-century life. For example, the growing number of women in the workforce demands more thought to maternity (and paternity) benefits. In addition, it should be clear by now that mass incarceration of drug users does little to help individuals and societies cope with the increasingly easy availability of narcotics and the tendency to use them by those struggling to cope with the quickening pace of change. What percentage of violent crime today is directly related to abuse of drugs and alcohol, and what's the cost to society—material and in terms of social cohesion—of continuing to ignore the need for large-scale substance abuse treatment? All societies will also need more effective approaches to the treatment of mental illness.

Studies show that more than 2 million Americans are dependent on medication and street drugs known as opioids, painkillers that mimic the effects of opium. Of the more than 52,000 drug overdose deaths in the United States in 2015, more than 63 percent involved an opioid. In August 2017, the Trump administration pledged "to use all appropriate authority to respond to the opioid emergency." In October 2017, Trump declared the opioid crisis a "public health emergency," but by not formally declaring a "national emergency," his announcement failed to make available federal funding to deal with the problem.[23] Identifying problems is an important first step. Solving them takes a much more significant commitment.

There are broader questions for policymakers to consider. It's human nature to gravitate toward other people who seem to share something in common with us. In school, we join subgroups of kids with whom we feel comfortable. As adults, we seek out places to live where we feel we'll be welcomed by people who share our values. For news and information about the world, we turn to television channels, radio stations, and Internet sites that offer views that we expect will line up with our opinions. This is the "filter bubble" that has become a toxic habit of our daily lives.

For the sake of social cohesion, there is value in "nudging" people together. In countries around the world, political leaders try to bolster their popularity by playing one group of people off another. If your goal is to boost your popularity with a segment of the population, that's a smart political tactic. But if your goal is to promote a stronger, healthier society that will make your country safer and more prosperous, it's a cynical and dangerous habit. Governments around the world have a lousy track record in the field of "social engineering," and their clumsiness often produces anger rather than unity. But given the ongoing political, technological, and social changes detailed in this book, the stoking of division is the shortcut to catastrophe. There are ways that government can create incentives that bring different types of people together—at school, in the workplace, and in public spaces.

BEYOND GOVERNMENT

Yet all these solutions, large and small, can only be implemented in societies that have a government willing and able to experiment, institutions capable of executing the best-laid plans, and a population of people who believe they share some basic values with their fellow citizens, even if it's only a common patriotism.[24] For these and other reasons, better government isn't the only answer, or even necessarily the most important. There are things private organizations can do, and are doing, particularly if government can help.

In January 2018, Lany Fink, founder of investment firm BlackRock, made headlines with a public announcement that the private sector must do more to serve communities. In an open letter to the CEOs of companies in which his firm invests, he warned that "Society is demanding that companies, both public and private, serve a social purpose. . . . Companies must benefit all of their stakeholders, including shareholders, employees, customers, and all the communities in which they operate."*

One of the most active participants in experiments with private-sector involvement in meeting the evolving needs of citizens is Facebook chairman Mark Zuckerberg. In February 2017, Zuckerberg outlined his ambitions in a blog post addressed to Facebook's 1.7 billion users.[25] The most succinct statement of his goal is to "develop the social infrastructure to give people the power to build a global community that works for all of us." The longer version includes plans to:

help people build supportive communities that strengthen traditional institutions in a world where membership in these institutions is declining, . . . help people build a safe community that prevents harm, helps during crises and rebuilds afterwards in a world where anyone across the world can affect us, . . . help people build an informed community that exposes us to new ideas and builds common understanding in a world where every person has a voice, . . . help people build a civically-engaged commu-

---

*www.blackrock.com/corporate/en-no/investor-relations/larry-fink-ceo-letter

nity in a world where participation in voting sometimes includes less than half our population, . . . [and] help people build an inclusive community that reflects our collective values and common humanity from local to global levels, spanning cultures, nations and regions in a world with few examples of global communities.

His essay looked beyond national governments. Progress, he wrote, "now requires humanity coming together not just as cities or nations, but also as a global community."[26]

These are grandiose aspirations. More specifically, Zuckerberg proposes to create stronger "safety infrastructure." Facebook already offers Safety Check, which allows users to connect with one another after emergencies, when governments, local and national, are sometimes overwhelmed. He also says he wants to experiment with programs based on artificial intelligence that can expose both "fake news"—an obvious danger to democracy—and efforts to recruit terrorists across the network. Zuckerberg faced intense criticism throughout 2017 for his company's failure to prevent Russians from using Facebook to disseminate phony information during their campaign to disrupt the 2016 U.S. election. But he is absolutely right about the private sector's opportunity to provide services that government can't or won't.

In addition, in San Francisco, we've seen companies like Facebook, Airbnb, Salesforce, and others move into the business of providing affordable housing.[27] Internet access is becoming an increasingly essential service, and companies like Google Fiber and Webpass, a wireless home broadband provider that

Google has acquired, have provided infrastructure and access for cities across the United States. In parts of the world where access is a much bigger challenge, Facebook has partnered with Samsung, Nokia, Qualcomm, Ericsson, MediaTek, and Opera Software to form Internet.org, a project designed to provide low-cost Internet access to parts of the world plagued with poor infrastructure. According to Zuckerberg, the venture has used its carrier-subsidized Free Basics app and Express Wi-Fi hubs to expand from 3 million new Internet users in July 2014 to 40 million by November 2016, with hopes to use satellites and solar-powered drones to expand that number further.[28]

AOL cofounder Steve Case and J. D. Vance, author of *Hillbilly Elegy*, a bestselling book about lost jobs in middle America, have created an investment fund called "Rise of the Rest," which will invest in American communities hard hit by globalization's impact on U.S. industry. The fund includes some of the wealthiest and most influential men and women in American business among its partners and investors. Crucially, Case and Vance also say they want to create networks of entrepreneurship, a Silicon Valley–like ecosystem that will connect entrepreneurs in small towns with one another and with those who can finance their best ideas. AT&T has broken new ground in worker education and retraining, a crucial resource for both employers and employees in an increasingly automated world. Workers in the company have access to a database called "career intelligence," which shows them where jobs are available in other parts of the company and what skills are required to fill them. The company then offers short courses that provide "nanodegrees," certifications that they have developed for particular skill sets. Employees who demonstrate an interest in continued learning are provided with funding for university coursework relevant to their areas of interest. If employees do not show interest, this is noted on their employment records. Workers keep a career profile that tracks their training and accomplishments. Employees benefit by gaining access to exactly the skills they need to adapt and succeed in the workplace. Employers gain by simplifying their hiring needs.[29]

But what about a child's education, particularly in places where governments don't provide it. Canadian Tariq Fancy is founder of the Rumie Initiative, an ambitious nonprofit project designed to give children in developing countries a chance to learn.[30] I met Tariq in February 2017, and he explained how Rumie provides children who live in areas with limited or no access to education, including refugee camps, with tablets preloaded with textbooks, interactive lessons, and other teaching tools. An article he wrote called "From Books to Bytes: A Learning Revolution for the Poor" explains how the smart use of crowdsourcing technology can help people in the Arctic Circle use their computers to help Syrian refugees living in camps in Turkey get an education.[31] This is not a large corporation funding a social responsibility program—though some of those projects can be important and impactful as well. This is one nonprofit with a big idea to provide crucial services for people that government cannot or will not reach, and to provide them with access to knowledge and skills they would never get in any other way.

There are plenty of examples of innovation coming from the developing world. For example, M-Pesa, a mobile payment system based in Kenya, allows people to use their phones to move money. The program, created in 2007 by mobile giant Safaricom, is now used by more than half the country. Kenyans were using this mobile platform to withdraw and deposit money, send remittances, pay bills, and access credit for years before these services became common in wealthier countries. More than 100,000 Kenyans have since signed up for M-Tiba, a "health wallet" available on mobile devices that allows users to save for health care expenses.[32] These kinds of services are especially important in developing countries, where governments can't keep pace with the growing demands for basic services of fast-developing middle classes.

Then there's the challenge of protecting democracy. If governments can't do it, maybe the private sector can. Google and its sister company Jigsaw have offered free software designed to protect elections from malicious manipulation. In 2017, the two companies helped to defend a voter information website in the Netherlands against repeated cyberattacks ahead of Dutch national elections. Jigsaw then offered a "Protect Your Election" suite of products to help guard against attacks on elections in France, South Korea, and Germany.[33]

Universities are stepping into the breach as well, including by hiring workers in communities broken by poverty and violence. Following riots in the city of Baltimore in 2015, Johns Hopkins University and its health system hired hundreds of new workers from the worst affected neighborhoods through a $69 million job creation program called HopkinsLocal. The University of Chicago and University of Pennsylvania have experimented with similar initiatives in Chicago and Philadelphia, respectively.[34]

We can't rely on companies and private institutions to do everything that governments can't or won't do. Private actors have private interests; they serve the needs of a limited number of citizens, and they don't tend to last as long as institutions of government. Nor can local governments do it all. Many Americans have a "let the states decide" approach to a long list of issues, but for the most basic services, big differences in the ability and willingness of individual state governments to spend on education, public health, and public infrastructure exacerbate the problem of inequality of opportunity. This is true to varying degrees in every country. Yet private companies and institutions will be a crucial part of any serious effort to rewrite the social contract, because they can incubate ideas that governments won't and experiment in ways that government can't. This *will* make a difference. Companies can use the marketplace to find out what works and how people will respond to new ways of doing things.

These are a few examples of the thousands of ideas under development in companies around the world, ideas that can be adapted, reworked, scaled up, and reimagined. Individually, they can help limited numbers of people meet limited numbers of their needs. Collectively, they can encourage the innovations— whether created by policymakers, entrepreneurs, or activist visionaries—that can help limit the inevitable human damage inflicted as we advance nation by nation and community by community from the old world into the new.

CONCLUSION

No one voted for Donald Trump because he believed the United States was growing more secure and more prosperous. In a country where working-age men without jobs outnumber those with jobs by three to one and half of unemployed men take daily pain medication, a lot of people want "change."[1]

It's hard to imagine what sort of future Americans can expect if the fate of these people is ignored.

It's easy to find fault with populists like Trump. He's obnoxious, dishonest, and incompetent. But Donald Trump didn't create us vs. them. Us vs. them created Donald Trump, and those who dismiss his supporters are damaging the United States. There are good reasons to want smaller government. It's natural to fear that Washington spends too much money. There are reasons to worry that political correctness will kill freedom of speech and the birth of good ideas. There are plenty of Americans who care sincerely about people with preexisting medical conditions, but who fear that creation of another entitlement program will one day bankrupt the country, leaving government without money to cover anyone.

These people aren't stupid or mean-spirited. They don't hate poor people. Some of them are poor people. Many are Americans who fear that intellect too often overrides common sense, that their countrymen are more interested in what they can get than in who will pay, that too many politicians care more about universal ideals than about American workers and their families, and that the country they knew is fading away.

Many Trump voters, including those who once supported Barack Obama, backed him because they wanted change. Actual change, not the kind of change promised on campaign posters. There's a working class in the United States that really has seen more losses than gains from free trade. U.S. infrastructure is crumbling, the country's education system is underperforming, its health care system is in real trouble, and the U.S. penal system doesn't work. American soldiers have fought and died in wars that seemed to accomplish nothing and that were never adequately explained to the American people. These failures belong to the entire U.S. political establishment. Citizens feel lied to or ignored—by politicians, the mainstream media, the business elite, bankers, and public intellectuals. They believe the game is rigged in someone else's favor, and they have a point.

American democracy itself is eroding. Donald Trump was elected president with votes from 26.3 percent of eligible voters.

Hillary Clinton won 26.5 percent, but lost the electoral college. Yet here is the most revealing number: Nearly 45 percent of eligible American voters didn't vote at all. Some didn't show up because they felt their vote represented a drop in the ocean, and some lived in states where the outcome wasn't in doubt. Others felt that none of the candidates could or would make things better. But many of these more than 100 million eligible American voters just didn't believe the outcome mattered. Just 36.4 percent of those eligible voted in the 2014 midterm congressional elections.[2]

It gets worse. According to a study published in *The Journal of Democracy*, the share of young Americans who say it's important to live in a democratic country has dropped from 91 percent in the 1930s to 57 percent today. Fewer than one in three young Americans say that it's important to live in a democracy. In 1995, just one in sixteen Americans agreed that it would be "good" or "very good" to have military rule in the United States. In 2016, it was one in six.[3]

Trump has made things worse. He has further poisoned the attitudes of his followers toward government and the media, inflicted lasting damage on U.S. ties with close allies, and embarrassed the country before the world. Worst of all, he has deliberately pitted Americans against one another for political gain. We see the polarized electorate in Trump's own poll numbers. His supporters have backed him through conflicts and controversies that would have ended the careers of any other public official, and his detractors wouldn't thank him if he pulled them from a burning building.

But when critics focus on the man and ignore the underlying emergencies that lifted him to the White House, they exacerbate the American problem of us vs. them. They make it easier to build walls and harder to help those who need help most. It's much easier to mock Donald Trump, rail at his excesses, and caricature his backers than to work toward solutions to the problems that leave many convinced they have no future and that their fellow Americans don't care.

As in the United States, it's easy to demonize those Europeans who fear open borders as heartless racists who care nothing for refugees and hate Muslims. We can ignore those who say their governments have ceded too much power to bureaucrats in Brussels. But these people know that if they welcome unlimited numbers of migrants, they're inviting large numbers of people to risk their lives and those of their children to make the journey and that smaller European countries will struggle to manage the overflow. They're right that not all these migrants are truly refugees, and that encouraging so many to leave their home countries allows autocrats in North Africa and the Middle East to drive out those who don't support them. It is not racist to acknowledge that the best of intentions sometimes produce terrible consequences.

Further, democracy is undermined when growing numbers of the decisions that govern people's lives are made by people who don't stand for election within the borders of their countries. Attacking political demagogues like Beppe Grillo and Marine Le Pen is one thing. Dismissing the hopes and fears of those who turn to them exacerbates the problem of us vs. them and makes it more difficult to rework the European social contract in ways that both left and right can accept.

Challenges that are serious for the United States and Europe are even more daunting for developing countries. The introduction of automation and artificial intelligence into the workplace will create more turmoil for workers in wealthy countries, but it will be profoundly disruptive in the developing world, where there will be fewer factory jobs to pull less educated people from the countryside into the urban workforce. Governments without money to invest in technological innovation—and to upgrade education systems and retraining programs to help citizens profit from it—will create fewer opportunities for young people. Social unrest will test the resilience of governments, and political officials will stoke more conflict between us and them to protect their own power and influence.

The result will be a widening of the divide between wealthy countries and poor ones—and between rich and poor within each country. And if we focus mainly on the demagoguery of the populists who try to take advantage of these trends, we will only widen the gap between those who can afford to ignore them and those who can't.

There is another danger common to every nation on earth. Each year, human beings now produce more data than in every previous year combined.[4] The choices we make, particularly online, help algorithms understand our interests, wants, and needs better than our friends and families do. Add the reality that people are easy to influence. Fake news generated on the Internet shapes public perception in ways we still don't fully appreciate, and a coming wave of digitally sophisticated fake images and video will complicate things further. It's not difficult to imagine a world in which technical specialists looking to make money help politicians looking to gain power understand and manipulate us in ways that undermine the political influence of citizens in every country. Over time, people wise up. They become less easy to fool. But they can easily become more cynical, and that can lead them to turn their backs on politics altogether, leaving elections to be decided by the angriest and most opinionated.

In the meantime, there are choices to make. Build walls? Or rewrite the social contract? Both strategies can work in many countries, at least for a while. Both demand capable government with the resources to construct and sustain these systems. The construction of walls won't kill the idea of responsive government. It will simply create a form of digital apartheid that ensures some are well served while others aren't served at all. As in Israel. And, increasingly, as in the United States. Reinvention of the social contract is going to be politically impossible in many countries for many years to come. The sense of crisis isn't yet strong enough, because so many globalists continue to profit from the system as it is, and walls of various kinds will protect them, temporarily, from real danger. Things have to become much worse, particularly for the winners, before they can become better for everyone else. This is the ultimate failure of globalism.

Where and when it becomes possible to experiment, efforts to rewrite the social contract will work most easily in countries with relatively homogeneous societies, borders that face relatively little pressure, and the means to continually expand economic productivity. But this principle can work in any country where a positive political consensus is possible. Remaking the relationship between citizens and government is much more likely than the construction of walls to create lasting security and prosperity for the greatest number of people.

History and personal experience show that people give their best when the best is required of them. That day is coming sooner than we think. Even those who think they want war will change their minds when they see its costs. Human beings use their natural ingenuity to create the tools they need to survive. In this case, survival requires that we invent new ways to live together.

Necessity must again become the mother of invention.

ACKNOWLEDGMENTS

This book was born in Lexington, Virginia. Just before the 2016 U.S. presidential election, I spent a day at the Virginia Military Institute, the oldest state-supported military college in the United States. It's a great place to go to have your faith restored in America, because every acre of that campus offers a reminder that no matter how divided the country, when we set our minds to it, Americans are capable of instilling the sort of values in our young men and women that the world can be proud of. I was struck again and again by the school's emphasis on integrity and stewardship.

I took the tour, got a feel for the place, visited with cadets, and then gave a speech to the student body. I remember one cadet's question in particular—about trade. I had spoken about the importance of the Trans-Pacific Partnership (TPP). I argued that if our government backed away from it, China would fill the vacuum, creating longer-term problems for the United States.

The cadet said he was from West Virginia. He said there were no jobs there. Coal mines and factories were shut down. Families were fractured. People felt forgotten. He told me that his family opposed NAFTA and free trade generally. He wanted to know what he should tell them to change their minds on TPP.

I told them he shouldn't try to change their minds, that while I supported the deal, there was nothing about our system that made me believe that trade would help him, his family, or his community. It made sense for his family to oppose trade until people took the consequences of trade for families like his much more seriously.

That's not a very satisfying answer, but it's an honest one. For me, it felt like the beginning of a more ambitious answer about where the world is headed. I hope this book takes that answer a little further.

I'm grateful to a number of deep and provocative thinkers for helping me get my head around these issues. To Carl Bildt, Borge Brende, Vint Cerf, Jared Cohen, Ivo Daalder, Mohamed el-Erian, Catherine Fieschi, Adam Grant, Richard Haass, Wolfgang Ischinger, Bob Kagan, Zach Karabell, Parag Khanna, Sallie Krawcheck, Christine Lagarde, David Lipton, David Miliband, Maziar Minovi, James Murdoch, Niko Pfund, Alec Ross, Kevin Rudd, Nouriel Roubini, Marci Shore, Doug Shuman, Nick Thompson, Enzo Viscusi, Steve Walt, and Fareed Zakaria. And I keep thinking about James Chace and David Fromkin, whose opinions frame so many of my own. I miss them. A lot.

My profound appreciation also to our whip-smart team of political scientists at Eurasia Group. If I've had any success as a "global thinker," whatever that means, it's because of how much they've taught me, the ways in which they bring their disparate backgrounds to their work, how much they've challenged me, and how much we've learned together when we don't have the answers (or think we do . . . and find out we don't). In particular, my thanks to Andrew Bishop, Chris Garman, Ayham Kamel, Alex Kazan, Dan Kerner, Cliff Kupchan, Evan Medeiros, Tsveta Petrova, Mij Rahman, and Karthik Sankaran, who went beyond the call of duty to help with the research that went into *Us vs. Them*. Anahita Arora offered many important ideas and generous support for this book.

I'd call Willis Sparks my alter ego, but after fourteen years and six books, there's much more id involved. He's absolutely brilliant, and I honestly can't remember what it was like to work without him. Leon Levy, Gabe Lipton, and Edana Ng round out our crack research team, our inner circle on everything global, and they're a pleasure to work with.

Alex Sanford started off working with me on research, then communications and media, and now runs a whole damned media company. She's still on point making sure the book gets out there, with the critical support of Erina Aoyama and Alex Gibson, whom we both deeply admire. My warmest thanks to Kim Tran and Ester Bakalli, who keep me sane on a daily basis. And Sarah Henning, my chief of staff, who makes the implausible look effortless. Because she's damned smart.

I'm grateful for my publishing team. Adrian Zackheim has been my partner in publishing crime for a decade now. Given that nobody reads books anymore, that's indeed what it feels like, yet we still manage to stay in business. He must know a guy who knows a guy. We both appreciate the work of Will Weisser and Bria Sandford. Four tips of the cap to Tara Gilbride and Stefanie Rosenbloom at Portfolio and to Allison McLean and Liz Hazelton at Amplify Partners, our aptly named publicists. Plus my agent, Rafe Sagalyn. (Having a book agent feels kind of globalist.)

To my chickie, Ann; my brother, Rob; my sister-in-law, Elizabeth; and my adorable new niece, Elisa.

And Moose the dog. For him, it's been a couple decades since I've written a book. Poor little bastard.

NOTES

CHAPTER 1: WINNERS AND LOSERS

1. Lucy Williamson, "Marine Le Pen's French Presidential Campaign Goes Lift-Off," BBC, February 5, 2017, www.bbc .com/news/world-europe-38874070.
2. Emma Luxton, "Which Countries Are Most Optimistic?," World Economic Forum, February 9, 2016, www.weforum.org/agenda /2016/02/which-countries-are-most-optimistic/.
3. Michael Wolff, "Ringside with Steve Bannon at Trump Tower," *Hollywood Reporter*, November 8, 2016, www.hollywoodreporter .com/news/steve-bannon-trump-tower-interview-trumps -strategist-plots-new-political-movement-948747.
4. "What Worries the World," Ipsos Public Affairs, July 2017, www .ipsos.com/sites/default/files/2017-08/What_worries_the_world -July-2017.pdf.
5. This respite did not apply to Italy, which continues to receive growing numbers of asylum seekers arriving by boat from North Africa.
6. Paul Carrel, "Germany's 2016 Trade Surplus Sets New Record," Reuters, February 9, 2017, http://uk.reuters.com/article/uk -germany-economy-trade-idUKKBN15O0NA.
7. Dani Rodrik, "Populism and the Economics of Globalization," Harvard University, August 2017, https://drodrik.scholar.harvard

.edu/files/dani-rodrik/files/populism_and_the_economics_of
_globalization.pdf.

8. Michael Hicks and Srikant Devaraj, "The Myth and Reality
of Manufacturing in America," Conexus Indiana, Ball State
University, April 2017, http://conexus.cberdata.org/files
/MfgReality.pdf.

9. Michael Chui, James Manyika, and Mehdi Miremadi, "Where
Machines Could Replace Humans—And Where They Can't
(Yet)," *McKinsey Quarterly*, July 2016, www.mckinsey.com
/business-functions/digital-mckinsey/our-insights/where
-machines-could-replace-humans-and-where-they-cant-yet.

10. "The American Middle Class Is Losing Ground," Pew Research
Center, December 9, 2015, www.pewsocialtrends.org/2015/12/09
/the-american-middle-class-is-losing-ground/.

11. Josh Zumbrun, "Economists Doubt the U.S. Can Regain Many of
the Factory Jobs Lost in Recent Decades," *Wall Street Journal*,
December 8, 2016, www.wsj.com/articles/economists-doubt
-the-u-s-can-regain-many-of-the-factory-jobs-lost-in-recent
-decades-1481209203.

12. Nicholas Eberstadt, "Our Miserable 21st Century," *Commentary*,
February 15, 2017, www.commentarymagazine.com/articles/our
-miserable-21st-century/.

13. "The Employment Situation—October 2017," U.S. Bureau of
Labor Statistics, November 3, 2017, www.bls.gov/news.release
/pdf/empsit.pdf.

14. Philip Bump, "Donald Trump Will Be President Thanks to
80,000 People in These Three States," *Washington Post*, December
1, 2016, www.washingtonpost.com/news/the-fix/wp/2016/12/01
/donald-trump-will-be-president-thanks-to-80000-people-in
-three-states/?utm_term=.ffc93808cc25.

15. Rodrik, "Populism and the Economics of Globalization."

16. "Boris Johnson: EU Makes Net Migration Target 'Impossible,'"
BBC, May 11, 2016, www.bbc.com/news/uk-politics-eu-referendum
-36265464.

17. John Sides, "Race, Religion, and Immigration in 2016," Voter
Study Group, June 2017, www.voterstudygroup.org/reports/2016
-elections/race-religion-immigration-2016.

18. Lee Drutman, "Political Divisions in 2016 and Beyond: Tensions Between and Within the Two Parties," Democracy Fund, Voter Study Group, June 2017, http://d.pr/f/B6JTY6.

19. "United Kingdom," International Monetary Fund, www.imf.org /en/Countries/GBR#ataglance and www.migrationobservatory .ox.ac.uk/resources/briefings/migrants-in-the-uk-an-overview/#kpl.

20. Angelique Chrisafis, "Macron Pledges Pragmatism and Cooperation with Post-Brexit Britain," *Guardian*, June 21, 2017, www.theguardian.com/world/2017/jun/21/exclusive-macron -pledges-pragmatism-and-cooperation-with-post-brexit-britain.

21. Jon Rogers and Monika Pallenberg, "Merkel's Economic Adviser Savages Her Migrant Policy and Says It Will Cost Germany €340BN," *Express* (UK), February 21, 2017, www.express.co.uk /news/world/770084/Angela-Merkel-open-door-migrant-policy -Hans-Werner-Sinn.

22. "Asylum and First Time Asylum Applicants," Eurostat, http:// ec.europa.eu/eurostat/en/web/products-datasets/-/MIGR _ASYAPPCTZA.

23. Rick Noack, "Sexual Assaults Challenge Germany's Welcoming Attitude Toward Refugees," *Washington Post*, January 6, 2016, www.washingtonpost.com/news/worldviews/wp/2016/01/06 /sexual-assaults-challenge-germanys-welcoming-attitude-toward -refugees/?utm_term=.473cf42b6edf.

24. Jacopo Barigazzi, "Brussels Takes On (Most of the) Visegrad Group over Refugees," *Politico*, June 12, 2017, www.politico.eu/article /brussels-takes-on-most-of-the-visegrad-group-over-refugees/.

25. David Chazan, "West Europeans Want End to Open Borders," *Telegraph*, July 11, 2015, www.telegraph.co.uk/news/worldnews /europe/eu/11734074/West-Europeans-want-end-to-open-borders .html.

26. Ariel Malka and Yphtach Lelkes, "In a New Poll, Half of Republicans Say They Would Support Postponing the 2020 Election if Trump Proposed It," August 10, 2017, www .washingtonpost.com/news/monkey-cage/wp/2017/08/10/in-a-new -poll-half-of-republicans-say-they-would-support-postponing-the -2020-election-if-trump-proposed-it/?utm_term=.4849aadbbaed.

27. "Filter bubble" is a term coined by Internet activist Eli Pariser.

28. Thomas Piketty, Emmanuel Saez, and Gabriel Zucman, "Distributional National Accounts: Methods and Estimates for the United States," Working Paper 22945, National Bureau of Economic Research, December 2016, https://eml.berkeley .edu/~saez/Piketty-Saez-ZucmanNBER16.pdf.

29. Rodrik, "Populism and the Economics of Globalization."

30. Rick Gladstone, "Displaced Population Hit Record in '16, U.N. Says," *New York Times*, June 19, 2017, www.nytimes.com/2017/06 /19/world/middleeast/displaced-people-united-nations-global -trends.html?mcubz=0.

31. Philip Bump, "Most Americans Don't Want the Wall, Don't Think Mexico Will Pay for It and Don't Believe It Will Happen," *Washington Post*, August 25, 2017, www.washingtonpost.com /news/politics/wp/2017/08/25/most-americans-dont-want-the-wall -dont-think-mexico-will-pay-for-it-and-dont-believe-it-will -happen/?utm_term=.e58ccf7b1d59.

32. Maimuna Majumder, "Higher Rates of Hate Crimes Are Tied to Income Inequality," *Five Thirty Eight*, January 23, 2017, https:// fivethirtyeight.com/features/higher-rates-of-hate-crimes-are -tied-to-income-inequality.

33. Deborah Hardoon, "Inequality and Violence," *Policy and Practice* blog, Oxfam, September 21, 2016, http://policy-practice .oxfam.org.uk/blog/2016/09/inequality-and-violence; "'It Has Been Proven, Less Inequality Means Less Crime,'" World Bank, September 5, 2014, www.worldbank.org/en/news/feature/2014/09 /03/latinoamerica-menos-desigualdad-se-reduce-el-crimen.

34. https://defence.pk/pdf/threads/russian-defence-budget-set-to -drop-by-12.457858/

35. Kate Taylor, "This Map Shows Where You're Most Likely to Lose Your Job to Robots," *Business Insider*, May 3, 2017, www .businessinsider.fr/us/map-shows-most-job-will-be-lost-to -automation-2017-5/.

36. Daron Acemoglu and Pascual Restrepo, "Robots and Jobs: Evidence from US Labor Markets," Working Paper 23285, National Bureau of Economic Research, March 2017, www.nber .org/papers/w23285.

37. Claire Cain Miller, "Evidence That Robots Are Winning the Race for American Jobs," *New York Times*, March 28, 2017, www

.nytimes.com/2017/03/28/upshot/evidence-that-robots-are
-winning-the-race-for-american-jobs.html.

38. Venessa Wong, "In 18 Years, a College Degree Could Cost about
$500,000," BuzzFeed News, March 17, 2017, www.cnbc.com/2017
/03/17/in-18-years-a-college-degree-could-cost-about-500000.html.

39. Zack Friedman, "Student Loan Debt in 2017: A $1.3 Trillion
Crisis," *Forbes*, February 21, 2017, www.forbes.com/sites
/zackfriedman/2017/02/21/student-loan-debt-statistics-2017
/#572d6b625dab.

40. Cain Miller, "Evidence That Robots Are Winning the Race for
American Jobs."

CHAPTER 2: WARNING SIGNS

1. Umair Haque, "The Protests and the Metamovement," *Harvard
Business Review*, October 4, 2011, https://hbr.org/2011/10/the
-protests-and-the-metamovem and www.theguardian.com
/world/2011/may/15/arab-spring-tunisia-the-slap.

2. "Egypt's Mubarak Resigns After 30-Year Rule," CNN, February
11, 2011, www.cnn.com/2011/WORLD/africa/02/11/egypt
.revolution/index.html.

3. Tim Gaynor, "Gaddafi Caught like a 'Rat' in a Drain,
Humiliated and Shot," Reuters, October 21, 2011, www.reuters
.com/article/us-libya-gaddafi-finalhours/gaddafi-caught-like
-rat-in-a-drain-humiliated-and-shot-idUSTRE79K43S20111021.

4. "Syria. Events of 2016," Human Rights Watch, www.hrw.org
/world-report/2017/country-chapters/syria.

5. According to the OECD and UNESCO.

6. "People Living in Extreme Poverty," 2017 Atlas of Sustainable
Development Goals, World Bank, www.theatlas.com/charts
/SJG3LerCg.

7. Benjamin Haas, "China Riot Police Seal Off City Centre After
Smog Protesters Put Masks on Statues," *Guardian*, December 12,
2016, www.theguardian.com/world/2016/dec/12/china-riot-police
-seal-off-city-centre-after-smog-protesters-put-masks-on-statues.

8. Christian Göbel and Lynette Ong, "Social Unrest in China,"
Europe China Research and Advice Network, 2012, www
.chathamhouse.org/sites/files/chathamhouse/public/Research/

Asia/1012ecran_gobelong.pdf; Michael Wines, "Chinese Street Vendor Dispute Expands into Violent Melee," *New York Times*, June 12, 2011, www.nytimes.com/2011/06/13/world/asia/13china .html.

9. "Timeline of Gezi Park Protests," *Hürriyet Daily News*, June 6, 2013, www.hurriyetdailynews.com/timeline-of-gezi-park -protests-.aspx?pageID=238&nID=48321&NewsCatID=341.

10. Tom McCarthy and Matthew Weaver, "US on Turkey Protests: 'Vast Majority of the Protesters Have Been Peaceful,'" *Guardian*, June 3, 2013, www.theguardian.com/world/middle-east-live/2013 /jun/03/turkey-protester-killed-live.

11. Peter Beaumont, "Erdogan Issues Stark 'Final Warning' to Turkey's Gezi Park Protesters," *Guardian*, June 14, 2013, www .theguardian.com/world/2013/jun/13/turkey-gezi-park-protesters.

12. Recep Bozlagan, "The Local Elections in Turkey and Their Importance to Turkish Politics," Al-Jazeera Centre for Studies, October 27, 2013, http://studies.aljazeera.net/en/reports/2013/10 /2013102483930393904.html.

13. Constanze Letsch, "A Year After the Protests, Gezi Park Nurtures the Seeds of a New Turkey," *Guardian*, May 28, 2014, www.theguardian.com/world/2014/may/29/gezi-park-year-after -protests-seeds-new-turkey.

14. Esther Fuentes and Rachael Hilderbrand, "The Role of Pro-Impeachment Protests in Brazil's Uncertain Future," Council on Hemispheric Affairs, March 15, 2016, www.coha.org/the-role-of -pro-impeachment-protests-in-brazils-uncertain-future/#_ftn2 and www.reuters.com/article/us-brazil-protest/police-detain -17-in-sao-paulo-bus-fare-protest-idUSKCN0UR05H20160113.

15. Paul O'Keeffe, "Ethiopia Crackdown on Student Protests Taints Higher Education Success," *Guardian*, May 22, 2014, www .theguardian.com/global-development/poverty-matters/2014/may /22/ethiopia-crackdown-student-protest-education.

16. "'Such a Brutal Crackdown.' Killings and Arrests in Response to Ethiopia's Oromo Protests," Human Rights Watch, June 15, 2016, www.hrw.org/report/2016/06/15/such-brutal-crackdown/killings -and-arrests-response-ethiopias-oromo-protests.

17. www.cia.gov/library/publications/the-world-factbook/geos/et.html

18. "Ethiopia's Key: Young People and the Demographic Dividend," Population Reference Bureau, December 2014, www.prb.org /pdf15/ethiopia-demographic-dividend-factsheet.pdf.

19. Shaun Walker and Alec Luhn, "Opposition Leader Alexei Navalny Detained amid Protests Across Russia," *Guardian*, March 27, 2017, www.theguardian.com/world/2017/mar/26/opposition -leader-alexei-navalny-arrested-amid-protests-across-russia.

20. "Corruption," Levada Center, April 21, 2017, www.levada.ru/en /2017/04/21/corruption/.

21. Eleazer Corpuz and Patrick Caughill, "In the Developing World, Two-Thirds of Jobs Could Be Lost to Robots," World Economic Forum, November 14, 2016, www.weforum.org/agenda/2016/11 /in-the-developing-world-two-thirds-of-jobs-could-be-lost -to-robots.

22. Chris Bryant and Elaine He, "The Robot Rampage," Bloomberg, January 8, 2017, www.bloomberg.com/gadfly/articles/2017-01-09 /the-robot-threat-donald-trump-isn-t-talking-abou.

23. "2017 Edelman Trust Barometer: Trust and the CEO," Edelman, www.ifac.org/system/files/uploads/Comms/Day%201%20 -%20Trust%20Barometer%20-%20Justin%20Blake.pdf.

24. "Saudis 'to Tighten Curbs on Foreign Workers' in Local Jobs Push," *National* (UAE)/Reuters, March 21, 2017, www .thenational.ae/world/saudis-to-tighten-curbs-on-foreign -workers-in-local-jobs-push-1.18087.

25. To be wonky about it, this measure is based on a study by Eurasia Group, the political risk consultancy I founded in 1998. Response capacity is based on two elements: state capacity and innovation policy. State capacity itself is defined as a composite of measures of bureaucratic autonomy, bureaucratic skill and capacity, party institutionalization, rule of law, and regime legitimacy. Our Innovation Policy Index comprises metrics of research and development incentives, human capital and infrastructure investment, policies affecting technological adoption, economic development targets, intellectual property laws, informal sector activity, and labor market regulations. It is measured based on a combination of Eurasia Group analyst surveys and external data.

CHAPTER 3: FAULT LINES

1. Sean Gossel, "How Corruption Is Fraying SA's Social and Economic Fabric," *Mail and Guardian*, July 13, 2017, https://mg .co.za/article/2017-07-13-how-corruption-is-fraying-south-africas -social-and-economic-fabric.

2. Sean Gossel, "Violent SA Protests Surging on Endemic Graft. But Here's How to Fix It," BizNews, July 13, 2017, www.biznews .com/thought-leaders/2017/07/13/violent-sa-protests-surging-graft/.

3. "Mexico Expels North Korean Ambassador over Nuclear Tests," Reuters, September 7, 2017, www.reuters.com/article/us -northkorea-mexico/mexico-expels-north-korean-ambassador -over-nuclear-tests-idUSKCN1BI2ZV.

4. These are the most recent available estimates, as of 2017. There is no reason to believe there has been a dramatic reduction in poverty over the past seven years.

5. "The Commitment to Reducing Inequality Index," Development Finance International/Oxfam, July 2017, http://policy-practice .oxfam.org.uk/publications/the-commitment-to-reducing -inequality-index-a-new-global-ranking-of-governments-620316.

6. About 10 percent of Egypt's 90 million people are Christians, a group that Muslim radicals have long treated as "them."

7. Peter Schwartzstein, "Forget ISIS, Egypt's Population Boom Is Its Biggest Threat," *Newsweek*, March 20, 2017, www.newsweek.com /2017/03/31/egypt-population-birth-rate-food-water-shortage-isis -terrorism-sissi-570953.html.

8. Ruth Michaelson, "'We Want Bread': Subsidy Cut Sparks Protests Across Egypt," *Guardian*, March 8, 2017, www.theguardian.com /world/2017/mar/08/egypt-protests-we-want-bread-subsidy-cut.

9. www.globalsecurity.org/military/world/egypt/labor.htm

10. "Saudi Head of Religious Police Criticises Agents for Handling of 'Nail Polish' Row," *Telegraph*, June 7, 2012, www.telegraph .co.uk/news/worldnews/middleeast/saudiarabia/9316616/Saudi -head-of-religious-police-criticises-agents-for-handling-of-nail -polish-row.html.

11. Kelly McLaughlin, "Woman Who Sparked Outrage by Walking Through Saudi Village in a T-shirt and Short Skirt Is Arrested by Police," *Daily Mail*, July 18, 2017, www.dailymail.co.uk/news

/article-4707358/Woman-wore-short-skirt-Saudi-Arabia-arrested
.html#ixzz4s7d9h86r.

12. Spencer Dale, "New Economics of Oil," BP/Society of Business
Economists Annual Conference, London, October 13, 2015, www
.bp.com/content/dam/bp/pdf/speeches/2015/new-economics-of
-oil-spencer-dale.pdf.

13. The Lava Jato (Car Wash) scandal began in March 2014 when a
senior official at Petrobras, Brazil's state oil company, was implicated
in a money laundering investigation. In a bid for leniency, he
confessed that companies awarded contracts by Petrobras had
diverted cash into political slush funds. Billions of dollars in bribes
were revealed, and some of the most powerful players in Brazilian
politics and business, including two former presidents, have been
implicated.

14. Shannon O'Neil, "Automation Is Changing Latin America Too,"
Council on Foreign Relations, March 7, 2017, www.cfr.org/blog
/automation-changing-latin-america-too.

15. Michael Rubin, "More Evidence of Erdogan's Referendum
Rigging," *Newsweek*, April 20, 2017, www.newsweek.com
/michael-rubin-more-evidence-erdogans-referendum-rigging
-586730.

16. "Jakarta Protests: Muslims Turn Out in Force Against Christian
Governor Ahok," AFP/*Guardian*, December 2, 2016, www
.theguardian.com/world/2016/dec/02/jakarta-protests-muslims
-against-christian-governor-ahok.

17. Emma Allen, "Analysis of Trends and Challenges in the
Indonesian Labor Market," ADB Papers on Indonesia 16, Asian
Development Bank, March 2016, www.adb.org/sites/default/files
/publication/182935/ino-paper-16-2016.pdf.

18. Mari Marcel Thekaekara, "The Murder of Journalist Gauri
Lankesh Shows India Descending into Violence," *Guardian*,
September 7, 2017, www.theguardian.com/commentisfree/2017
/sep/07/gauri-lankesh-murder-hindu-extremists-hate-crime
-minorities.

19. Nita Bhalla, "The Party is Over for India's 'Presstitutes,'"
Hindustan Times, April 29, 2017, www.hindustantimes.com
/opinion/the-party-is-over-for-india-s-presstitutes/story
-K2EEzHoeiFMl9LlXDnQdiI.html.

20. Soutik Biswas, "Why Inequality in India Is at Its Highest Level in 92 Years," BBC, September 12, 2017, www.bbc.com/news /world-asia-india-41198638.

21. "Sanitation in India: The Final Frontier," *Economist*, July 19, 2014, www.economist.com/news/asia/21607837-fixing-dreadful -sanitation-india-requires-not-just-building-lavatories-also -changing.

22. www.ft.com/content/49ddda7e-028a-11e7-aa5b-6bb07f5c8e12

23. "India Needs $1.5 Trillion for Infrastructure, Arun Jaitley Says," *Times of India*, June 26, 2016, http://timesofindia.indiatimes.com /business/india-business/India-needs-1-5-trillion-for -infrastructure-Arun-Jaitley-says/articleshow/52928773.cms.

24. Vibhuti Agarwal, "Indians Have the Worst Access to Safe Drinking Water in the World," *Wall Street Journal*, March 22, 2016, https://blogs.wsj.com/indiarealtime/2016/03/22/indians -have-the-worst-access-to-safe-drinking-water-in-the-world/.

25. "Why India Has a Water Crisis," *Economist*, May 25, 2016, www .economist.com/blogs/economist-explains/2016/05/economist -explains-11.

26. Rick Gladstone, "India Will Be Most Populous Country Sooner Than Thought, U.N. Says," *New York Times*, July 29, 2015, www .nytimes.com/2015/07/30/world/asia/india-will-be-most-populous -country-sooner-than-thought-un-says.html?_r=1.

27. "How Well-Off Is China's Middle Class?," ChinaPower, Center for Strategic and International Studies, http://chinapower.csis.org /china-middle-class/.

28. Morgan Winsor, "China's Pollution Crisis: Nearly Two-Thirds of Underground Water Is Graded Unfit for Human Contact, Report Says," *International Business Times*, June 4, 2015, www.ibtimes .com/chinas-pollution-crisis-nearly-two-thirds-underground -water-graded-unfit-human-1953442.

29. Rob Schmitz, "China's New Weapon Against Water Pollution: Its People," Marketplace, May 2, 2016, www.marketplace.org/2016/04 /27/world/chinas-new-weapon-against-water-pollution-its-people.

30. Beth Gardiner, "China's Surprising Solutions to Clear Killer Air," *National Geographic*, May 5, 2017, http://news.nationalgeographic .com/2017/05/china-air-pollution-solutions-environment-tangshan/.

31. *Wall Street Journal*, May 20, 2017, www.wsj.com/articles/chinas
-prosperity-eludes-a-generation-of-aging-workers-1494408607
?mod=e2tw.

32. Graham Allison, "America Second? Yes, and China's Lead Is
Only Growing," *Boston Globe*, May 22, 2017, www.bostonglobe
.com/opinion/2017/05/21/america-second-yes-and-china-lead
-only-growing/7G6szOUkTobxmuhgDtLD7M/story.html.

33. Bryant and He, "The Robot Rampage."

CHAPTER 4: WALLS

1. "The World Bank in West Bank and Gaza," World Bank, www
.worldbank.org/en/country/westbankandgaza/overview.

2. Hagai Amit, "Israel's Unemployment Rate Falls to Lowest Rate
in Decades," *Haaretz*, August 21, 2017, www.haaretz.com/israel
-news/business/1.808252.

3. www.cia.gov/library/publications/the-world-factbook/geos/is.html

4. "The Battle of Smoot-Hawley," *Economist*, December 18, 2008,
www.economist.com/node/12798595.

5. Dominic Rushe, "Smoot and Hawley, the Ghosts of Tariffs Past,
Haunt the White House," *Guardian*, January 29, 2017, www
.theguardian.com/us-news/2017/jan/29/smoot-hawley-tariffs
-protectionism-donald-trump.

6. Michael Hiltzik, *The New Deal: A Modern History* (New York:
Free Press, 2011).

7. Alonzo Hamby, *For the Survival of Democracy* (New York: Simon
and Schuster, 1994), p. 164.

8. "The Lessons of 1937," *Economist*, June 18, 2009, www.economist
.com/node/13856176.

9. Hiltzik, *The New Deal*.

10. Alan Boyd, "ASEAN Free Trade Still a Distant Notion," *Asia
Times*, September 6, 2017, www.atimes.com/article/asean-free-trade
-still-distant-notion/?utm_source=The+Daily+Brief&utm
_campaign=6a07b57bf7-EMAIL_CAMPAIGN_2017_09_06&utm
_medium=email&utm_term=0_1f8bca137f-6a07b57bf7-31500929.

11. Danny Lee and Chris Keegan, "Beyond GDPR: Data
Localization Laws Abroad," Beecher Carlson, www

.beechercarlson.com/company-news/beyond-gdpr-data
-localization-laws-abroad.

12. Turkey's President Erdogan insists these journalists are guilty of support for "terrorism."

13. Elana Beiser, "Turkey's Crackdown Propels Number of Journalists in Jail Worldwide to Record High," Committee to Protect Journalists, December 13, 2016, https://cpj.org/reports /2016/12/journalists-jailed-record-high-turkey-crackdown.php.

14. Ruth Michaelson, "Egypt Blocks Access to News Websites Including Al-Jazeera and Mada Masr," *Guardian*, May 25, 2017, www.theguardian.com/world/2017/may/25/egypt-blocks-access -news-websites-al-jazeera-mada-masr-press-freedom.

15. Shruti Dhapola, "Internet Shutdowns in India: Why It Is Bad for Modi's Digital India," *Indian Express*, March 27, 2017, http:// indianexpress.com/article/technology/tech-news-technology/internet -shutdowns-in-india-why-it-is-bad-for-modis-digital-india-4587416/.

16. "Cameroon Ends Internet Shutdown on Orders of President Paul Biya," BBC, April 21, 2017, www.bbc.com/news/world-africa -39665244.

17. Colin Daileda, "Turkey's Internet Censorship Is Starting to Look Like China's 'Great Firewall,'" Mashable, December 20, 2016, http://mashable.com/2016/12/19/turkey-blocks-tor-vpn -censorship/#lTzU2owatmqZ.

18. "Tor Blocked in Turkey as Government Cracks Down on VPN Use," Turkey Blocks, December 18, 2016, https://turkeyblocks.org /2016/12/18/tor-blocked-in-turkey-vpn-ban/.

19. "Iran Creates 'Halal Internet' to Control Online Information," Reporters Without Borders, September 6, 2016, https://rsf.org/en /news/iran-creates-halal-internet-control-online-information.

20. Emily Parker, "Russia Is Trying to Copy China's Approach to Internet Censorship," *Slate*, April 4, 2017, www.slate.com/articles /technology/future_tense/2017/04/russia_is_trying_to_copy _china_s_internet_censorship.html.

21. Andrew Kramer, "Russians Selectively Blocking Internet," *New York Times*, March 31, 2013, www.nytimes.com/2013/04/01 /technology/russia-begins-selectively-blocking-internet-content.html.

22. www.cnn.com/2017/11/25/world/russia-foreign-agents-law -media/index.html

23. Eva Hartog, "How a New Law Is Making It Difficult for Russia's Aggregators to Tell What's New(s)," *Moscow Times*, April 7, 2017, https://themoscowtimes.com/articles/how-a-new-law-is-making-it -difficult-for-russias-news-aggregators-to-tell-whats-going-on-57657.

24. "China to Further Tighten Its Internet Controls," Reuters, May 7, 2017, www.reuters.com/article/us-china-internet-idUSKBN1830AG ?utm_source=Fareed%27s+Global+Briefing&utm_campaign =43b5234f80-EMAIL_CAMPAIGN_2017_05_08&utm _medium=email&utm_term=0_6f2e93382a-43b5234f80-84041237.

25. "China's 'Great Cannon,'" *Washington Post*, April 11, 2015, www .washingtonpost.com/opinions/chinas-great-cannon/2015/04/11 /c926c718-dfa6-11e4-a1b8-2ed88bc190d2_story.html?utm_term =.c0aff575f6f1.

26. "China Invents the Digital Totalitarian State," *Economist*, December 17, 2016, www.economist.com/news/briefing/21711902 -worrying-implications-its-social-credit-project-china-invents -digital-totalitarian.

27. Kaya Yurieff, "This Robot Can 3D Print a Building in 14 Hours," CNN, May 2, 2017, http://money.cnn.com/2017/05/02/technology /3d-printed-building-mit/.

28. "More Neighbours Make More Fences," *Economist*, January 7, 2016, www.economist.com/blogs/graphicdetail/2016/01/daily-chart-5.

29. Nick Wingfield, "Oculus Founder Plots a Comeback with a Virtual Border Wall," *New York Times*, June 4, 2017, www .nytimes.com/2017/06/04/business/oculus-palmer-luckey-new -start-up.html?utm_source=newsletter&utm_medium=email &utm_campaign=newsletter_axiosam&stream=top-stories&_r=0.

30. "Golden door" is a reference to the Emma Lazarus poem featured on the Statue of Liberty.

31. Katie Beck, "Why Citizenship Is Now a Commodity," BBC, May 30, 2017, www.bbc.com/capital/story/20170530-why-citizenship -is-now-a-commodity.

32. Charles Blow, "The Self-Sort," *New York Times*, April 11, 2014, www.nytimes.com/2014/04/12/opinion/blow-the-self-sort.html?_r=0.

33. Dana Thompson Dorsey, "Segregation 2.0: The New Generation of School Segregation in the 21st Century," *Education and Urban Society* 45 (September 2013), pp. 533–547, http://journals.sagepub .com/doi/pdf/10.1177/0013124513486287.

34. Lindsay Dunsmuir, "Many Americans Have No Friends of Another Race: Poll," Reuters, August 8, 2013, www.reuters.com /article/us-usa-poll-race-idUSBRE97704320130808.

35. See summary article at Paul Taylor, "The Demographic Trends Shaping American Politics in 2016 and Beyond," Fact Tank, Pew Research Center, January 27, 2016, www.pewresearch.org/fact-tank /2016/01/27/the-demographic-trends-shaping-american -politics-in-2016-and-beyond/.

36. Richard North Patterson, "The Democrats' Demographic Dilemma," *Boston Globe*, February 14, 2017, www.bostonglobe.com /opinion/2017/02/14/the-democrats-demographic-dilemma /K1LM2FbTRdhk3FX1cGZG4H/story.html.

37. Adam Liptak, "Supreme Court Invalidates Key Part of Voting Rights Act," *New York Times*, June 25, 2013, www.nytimes.com /2013/06/26/us/supreme-court-ruling.html.

38. "New Voting Restrictions in America," Brennan Center for Justice, New York University School of Law, www.brennancenter .org/new-voting-restrictions-america.

39. The fourteen were Alabama, Arizona, Indiana, Kansas, Mississippi, Nebraska, New Hampshire, Ohio, Rhode Island, South Carolina, Tennessee, Texas, Virginia, and Wisconsin.

40. "Voting Laws Roundup 2017," Brennan Center for Justice, New York University School of Law, May 10, 2017, www .brennancenter.org/analysis/voting-laws-roundup-2017.

41. Justin Levitt, "A Comprehensive Investigation of Voter Impersonation Finds 31 Credible Incidents out of One Billion Ballots Cast," *Washington Post*, August 6, 2014, www .washingtonpost.com/news/wonk/wp/2014/08/06/a-comprehensive -investigation-of-voter-impersonation-finds-31-credible-incidents -out-of-one-billion-ballots-cast/?utm_term=.d825eaac36b3.

42. Ari Berman, "Trump's Commission on 'Election Integrity' Will Lead to Massive Voter Suppression," *Nation*, May 11, 2017, www .thenation.com/article/trumps-commission-on-election-integrity -will-lead-to-massive-voter-suppression/.

43. "India's ID System Is Reshaping Ties Between State and Citizens," *Economist*, April 12, 2017, www.economist.com/news /asia/21720609-long-they-have-mobile-signal-indias-id-system -reshaping-ties-between-state-and-citizens.

44. "China Invents the Digital Totalitarian State," *Economist*, December 17, 2016, www.economist.com/news/briefing/21711902 -worrying-implications-its-social-credit-project-china-invents -digital-totalitarian.

CHAPTER 5: NEW DEALS

1. John Helliwell, Richard Layard, and Jeffrey Sachs (eds.), "World Happiness Report 2017," Sustainable Development Solutions Network, New York, 2017, http://worldhappiness.report/ed/2017/.
2. The first government pension plan was introduced by Otto von Bismarck in imperial Germany. The world's first old-age social insurance plan was established in 1889. The retirement age was set at seventy.
3. "A Timeline of the Evolution of Retirement in the United States," Workplace Flexibility 2010, Georgetown University Law Center, http://scholarship.law.georgetown.edu/cgi/viewcontent.cgi?article =1049&context=legal.
4. Eduardo Porter, "Investments in Education May Be Misdirected," *New York Times*, April 2, 2013, www.nytimes.com/2013/04/03 /business/studies-highlight-benefits-of-early-education.html.
5. Rebecca Mead, "The Lessons of Mayor Bill De Blasio's Universal Pre-K Initiative," *New Yorker*, September 7, 2017, www .newyorker.com/news/daily-comment/the-lessons-of-mayor -bill-de-blasios-universal-pre-k-initiative.
6. Scott McDonald, "Businesses Can No Longer Avoid Becoming Political," *Harvard Business Review*, April 20, 2017, https://hbr.org /2017/04/businesses-can-no-longer-avoid-becoming-political.
7. "Equipping People to Stay Ahead of Technological Change," *Economist*, January 14, 2017, www.economist.com/news/leaders /21714341-it-easy-say-people-need-keep-learning-throughout -their-careers-practicalities.
8. Kevin Delaney, "The Robot That Takes Your Job Should Pay Taxes, Says Bill Gates," Quartz, February 17, 2017, https://qz.com /911968/bill-gates-the-robot-that-takes-your-job-should-pay-taxes/.
9. Lawrence Summers, "Robots Are Wealth Creators and Taxing Them Is Illogical," *Financial Times*, March 5, 2017, www.ft.com /content/42ab292a-000d-11e7-8d8e-a5e3738f9ae4.

10. Nils Pratley and Jill Treanor, "Mohamed El-Erian: 'We Get Signals That the System Is Under Enormous Stress,'" *Guardian*, May 13, 2017, www.theguardian.com/business/2017/may/13/mohamed-el-erian-signals-system-enormous-stress-global-capitalism.

11. Liz Alderman, "Feeling 'Pressure All the Time' on Europe's Treadmill of Temporary Work," *New York Times*, February 9, 2017, www.nytimes.com/2017/02/09/business/europe-jobs-economy-youth-unemployment-millenials.html?emc=edit_nn_20170209&nl=morning-briefing&nlid=75028914&te=1&_r=0.

12. Marie Preisler, "Disruption Shakes the Nordic Agreement Model," *Nordic Labour Journal*, May 19, 2017, www.nordiclabourjournal.org/i-fokus/in-focus-2017/sharing-economy-2017/article.2017-05-18.0607954247.

13. Maija Unkuri, "Will Finland's Basic Income Trial Help the Jobless?," BBC, January 16, 2017, www.bbc.com/news/world-europe-38593513.

14. Leonid Bershidsky, "A Robot Tax Is a Bad Idea," Bloomberg, January 23, 2017, www.bloomberg.com/view/articles/2017-01-23/why-benoit-hamon-s-idea-of-a-robot-tax-is-flawed.

15. Thomas Paine, "Agrarian Justice," www.ssa.gov/history/paine4.html.

16. Andrew Flowers, "What Would Happen if We Just Gave People Money?," *Five Thirty Eight*, April 25, 2016, http://fivethirtyeight.com/features/universal-basic-income/.

17. Stephen Kresge and Leif Wenar (eds.), *Hayek on Hayek: An Autobiographical Dialogue* (Chicago: University of Chicago Press, 1994).

18. Christine Emba, "Universal Basic Income," *Washington Post*, September 28, 2015, www.washingtonpost.com/news/in-theory/wp/2015/09/28/universal-basic-income-a-primer/?utm_term=.cbeee65e1209.

19. "Signing for Paradise to Come," *Economist*, June 4, 2016, www.economist.com/news/briefing/21699910-arguments-state-stipend-payable-all-citizens-are-being-heard-more-widely-sighing.

20. "The Social Contract," *Economist*, July 16, 2015, www.economist.com/news/special-report/21657613-two-big-simple-government-promisesof-home-and-comfortable-old-agehave-become-harder.

21. Jonathan Tepperman, "Brazil's Antipoverty Breakthrough," *Foreign Affairs*, January/February 2016, www.foreignaffairs.com /articles/brazil/2015-12-14/brazils-antipoverty-breakthrough.

22. Allen Cone, "Saudi Arabia Cuts Government Workers' Pay for First Time," UPI, September 27, 2016, www.upi.com/Saudi -Arabia-cuts-government-workers-pay-for-first-time /9441474985619/.

23. www.nytimes.com/2017/10/26/us/politics/trump-opioid-crisis .html

24. Seth Kaplan, "Horizontal Versus Vertical Social Cohesion: Why the Differences Matter," Global Dashboard, March 12, 2012, www.globaldashboard.org/2012/03/12/horizontal-versus-vertical -social-cohesion-why-the-differences-matter/.

25. Mark Zuckerberg, "Building Global Community," Facebook, February 16, 2017, www.facebook.com/notes/mark-zuckerberg /building-global-community/10154544292806634.

26. "I think today we need more global infrastructure in order to unlock a lot of the biggest opportunities and solve some of the biggest challenges. So when you're talking about spreading freedom or trade, or you're talking about fighting terrorism, where a civil war in one country leads to refugee crises across multiple continents, these are not typically problems any one country has the tools by itself to go solve. I think we have a responsibility as a technology company at a pretty big scale to see what we can do to push on that." Robert Safian, "Mark Zuckerberg on Fake News, Free Speech, and What Drives Facebook," *Fast Company*, April 11, 2017, www.fastcompany.com/40397297/mark-zuckerberg-on-fake -news-free-speech-and-what-drives-facebook.

27. Cory Weinberg, "Facebook, Airbnb, Salesforce Give $225K on S.F. Affordable Housing Ballot Measure," *San Francisco Business Times*, October 29, 2015, www.bizjournals.com/sanfrancisco/blog/real -estate/2015/10/facebook-airbnb-salesforce-affordable-housing.html.

28. Josh Constine, "Facebook Has Connected 40M People with Internet.org," TechCrunch, November 2, 2016, https://techcrunch .com/2016/11/02/omnipresent/.

29. "What Employers Can Do to Encourage Their Workers to Retrain," *Economist*, January 14, 2017, www.economist.com/news

/special-report/21714171-companies-are-embracing-learning-core
-skill-what-employers-can-do-encourage-their.

30. Paul Hunter, "Bringing Education to the World's Poor Children," *Toronto Star*, December 28, 2014, www.thestar.com/news/insight /2014/12/28/bringing_education_to_the_worlds_poor_children.html.

31. https://sosofancy.com/from-books-to-bytes-a-learning-revolution -for-the-poor-49b504b0245a

32. Dominic Omondi, "More Than Half of Kenyans Use M-Pesa, Says Report," *Standard Digital*, February 27, 2017, www .standardmedia.co.ke/business/article/2001230799/more-than -half-of-kenyans-use-m-pesa-says-report.

33. Eric Auchard and Toby Sterling, "Google and Sister Company to Offer Cyber Security to Election Groups," Reuters, March 21, 2017, www.reuters.com/article/us-cyber-election-idUSKBN16S166.

34. Sarah Larimer, "Hopkins Hires Hundreds in Baltimore, Seeking to Strengthen Community," *Washington Post*, March 9, 2017, www.washingtonpost.com/news/grade-point/wp/2017/03/09 /hopkins-hires-hundreds-in-baltimore-seeking-to-strengthen -community/?utm_term=.a7c8eb33842e.

CONCLUSION

1. Eberstadt, "Our Miserable 21st Century"; Gwynn Guilford and Preeti Varathan, "Nearly half of working-age American men who are out of the labor force are using painkillers daily," *Quartz*, September 7, 2017, https://qz.com/1070206/nearly-half-of-working -age-american-men-who-are-out-of-the-labor-force-are-using -painkillers-daily/.

2. Domenico Montanaro, Rachel Wellford, and Simone Pathe, "2014 Midterm Election Turnout Lowest in 70 Years," *PBS News Hour*, November 10, 2014, www.pbs.org/newshour/updates/2014 -midterm-election-turnout-lowest-in-70-years/.

3. Yascha Mounk, "Yes, American Democracy Could Break Down," *Politico*, October 22, 2016, www.politico.com/magazine/story/2016 /10/trump-american-democracy-could-break-down-214383.

4. Dirk Helbing et al., "Will Democracy Survive Big Data and Artificial Intelligence?," *Scientific American*, February 25, 2017, www.scientificamerican.com/article/will-democracy-survive-big -data-and-artificial-intelligence/.

INDEX

INDEX

INDEX

Henley, William Ernest, 7
Hillbilly Elegy (Vance), 157
Hoover, Herbert, 102
hukou system, 119–20
Hungary, 24–25

immigration, 115–18
    Brexit campaign and, 21
    economic arguments in favor of, 115–16
    European Union and, 20–21, 115, 118
    guest worker programs, 118
    job losses and fewer social services
        blamed on, 20–21
    number of refugees, in 2016, 28
    physical barriers to, 116–17
    of skilled and wealthy immigrants, 117–18
    Trump and, 19–20
    United States and, 19–20, 25–26, 28–29,
        115, 116, 118
    virtual walls, 117
income inequality, 5, 27–33, 97
    in Brazil, 54
    in China, 54, 92
    in developing countries, 51–52, 54–55
    in Egypt, 54–55, 65
    in European Union, 28
    in India, 54, 87
    in Indonesia, 54–55, 84
    in Mexico, 54
    in Nigeria, 54, 62–63
    rewriting social contract to address,
        139–40
    in Russia, 54–55, 82
    in Saudi Arabia, 54
    in South Africa, 54, 59–60
    in Turkey, 79
    in United States, 16–18, 27–28
    in Venezuela, 78
    violence and, 29–30
India, 86–90
    Aadhaar biometric identification system,
        125–27, 151, 152
    automation and, 45, 54, 89
    data localization laws, 106
    demographic vulnerability of, 54, 89
    economy of, 87–88, 90
    income inequality in, 54, 87
    infrastructure of, 88
    Internet, shutting down of, 108–9
    Jan Dhan, 151
    nongovernmental organizations, shutting
        down of, 108
    poverty in, 37, 87
    religious tensions in, 86–87, 90
    trust in government and its institutions, 53

us vs. them battles in, 86–87, 90
    water, access to, 88–89
Indian National Congress Party, 125
individual learning accounts, 142–43
individual retirement accounts, 140
Indonesia, 83–86
    automation and, 54, 85
    corruption in, 84
    data localization laws, 106
    demographic vulnerability of, 54, 85
    income inequality in, 54–55, 84
    poverty in, 84
    religious tensions in, 83–84
    trust in government and its institutions, 53
    us vs. them battles in, 83–84
information, access to, 106–14
    data localization laws, 106
    General Data Protection Regulation
        (European Union), 106
    Internet, shutting down or policing of,
        108–14
    journalists, jailing of, 106–7
    media outlets, shutting down of, 107
    nongovernmental organizations, shutting
        down of, 108
International Monetary Fund (IMF), 65, 66
Internet
    private sector initiatives to provide access
        to, 156–57
    shutting down or policing of, 108–14
Internet.org project, 157
Iran, 110
Irwin, Douglas, 102
ISIS, 30
Israel, 99–100

Jaitley, Arun, 88
Jan Dhan, 151
Jefferson, Thomas, 133–34
Jigsaw, 159
Johns Hopkins University, 159
Johnson, Boris, 21
Joko Widodo (Jokowi), 84, 85
Jordan, 117
journalists, jailing of, 106–7
Justice and Development Party, 78

Kautilya, 134
Kerry, John, 18
Kuti, Fela, 62

Lankesh, Gauri, 86
Lava Jato corruption scandal, 42, 73
Lenin, Vladimir, 35
Le Pen, Marine, 7–8, 13, 19, 24

INDEX